MIRABELLAFOOD

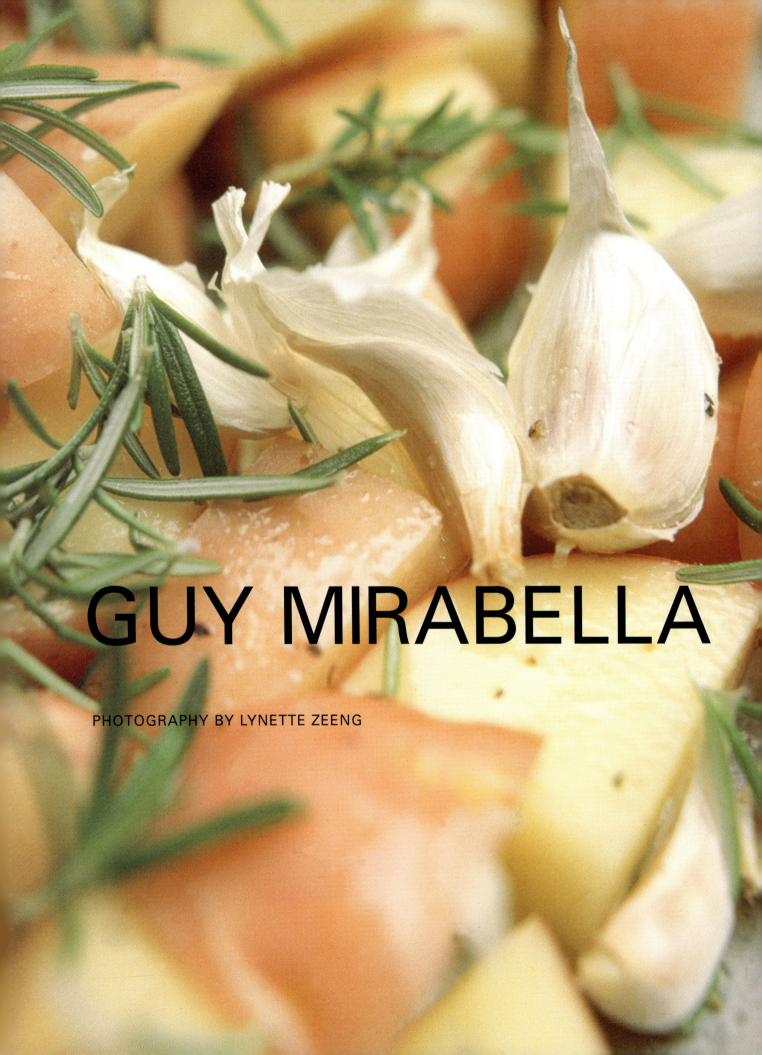

GUY MIRABELLA

PHOTOGRAPHY BY LYNETTE ZEENG

MIRABELLAFOOD
EATING SIMPLY, EATING WELL

Pan Macmillan Australia

First published 1999 in Macmillan by Pan Macmillan Australia Pty Limited
St Martins Tower, 31 Market Street, Sydney

Copyright © Guy Mirabella 1999

All rights reserved. No part of this book may be reproduced or transmitted in any form or by any means, electronic or mechanical, including photocopying, recording or by any information storage and retrieval system, without prior permission in writing from the publisher.

National Library of Australia
cataloguing-in-publication data:
    Mirabella, Guy
    Mirabella food: eating simply, eating well.
    ISBN 0 7329 0988 0.
    1. Cookery, Italian – Sicilian style. I. Title.

Designed by Guy Mirabella
Photography by Lynette Zeeng
Cover photo of Garlic and Rosemary Roast Potatoes by Lynette Zeeng
Author photo by Paul Perillo
Author photo art direction by Alex Greig
Typeset in Univers
Printed in Australia by the Australian Book Connection

CONTENTS

Acknowledgments vi

Introduction vii

Salads 1

Vegetables 17

Meat 37

Poultry 61

Fish and Seafood 85

Desserts 113

Index 135

ACKNOWLEDGMENTS

A book always starts off as a dream. The development of this project has been nurtured by a number of people whom I respect and admire and who have shared with me a passion for food. Their advice and support I value and I thank them from the bottom of my heart.

To Johanne, my travelling companion on an extraordinary journey, whose vision remains truthful and focused while I change, twist and turn. Her strength gives me the courage to go forward.

Our children, Danielle, Pam and Paul keep my spirit alive and fresh. There have been many times when I have been absent from their lives, and I am truly grateful for their understanding and love, and for their enthusiasm for the work I do and the food I cook.

To my father Diego, my mother Pina and my father-in-law Vincenzo, and to the memory of my mother-in-law Palmina, for their extravagance and generosity and their love of tradition, life and food.

To my brother and sisters and their families, and to Johanne's family, for their continuing support and many a get-together around the table. What wonderful memories we have.

Once again, my thanks and gratitude to Lynette Zeeng. Lynette not only took the photos but helped chop, stir and search for ingredients. Her eye once again performs its magic.

To my publisher Jane Curry for her guidance and wisdom and for gently pushing me in the right direction. To Peter Phillips, Paul Kenny and Mark Haldane whose commitment to the book has been invaluable. Thank you to my editor Elspeth Menzies for shaping the spirit of the words.

Thanks to Rick, Julie, Brett, Steve and Ray at Rick's Quality Meats in Frankston for their advice. And to Ian from the Mt Eliza Deli for his patience and guidance and Teresa Sfetkidis from Luv-a-Duck for her time and expertise.

To Consuelo Guinness for her advice and good taste. Her food delights and gives pleasure not just for the head and stomach but also for the soul.

INTRODUCTION

This book is inspired by a passion for the rustic peasant food of my Sicilian parents and life growing up on a farm on the Mornington Peninsula in Victoria. Our kitchen was always full of the scents, flavours and language of Sicily, and the produce we grew in our backyard—apples from our orchard, broccoli and cauliflower in winter and tomatoes and corn in summer.

At the end of a busy day my favourite way of unwinding is to prepare simple, fresh and delicious food that has a respect for ingredients and a fine balance of flavours: sizzling grilled vegetables; flavoursome marinated meat cooked over twigs of rosemary branches; chargrilled baby octopus and mussels, their beachy flavour enhanced by an Asian-inspired marinade; fresh seasonal berries drizzled with dry marsala and served on grilled panettone. Most of the recipes in this book can be cooked on the grill of a barbecue, or any type of chargrill, with flavours enhanced by simply basting with olive oil or fragrant marinades.

Family life and the enjoyment of food have always been intertwined for me, and many of the recipes in *Mirabella Food* have been inspired by food cooked by members of my family. I love preparing and eating food, whether it is for my family, sharing whatever news we have at the end of the day, or for friends, dining outside in the garden. Food has always filled me with pleasure and played an integral part in my life, and I have been fortunate to meet and work with people who share this passion.

Guy Mirabella 1999

SALADS

When the whole family gets together, my father Diego always prepares the salad we have with the main meal (see Diego's Mixed Green Salad on page 5). He rises from his chair at the end of the long kitchen table overflowing with rustic Sicilian food and begins his performance. There is always a briskness in his step as he approaches the large white enamelled bowl filled with torn green leaves and chopped cucumber, celery and radishes from his beloved garden. At the table he adds the tomatoes and with chunky fingers sprinkles salt and pepper over the lot. Next, he pours just enough olive oil to coat the leaves and give them a rich lustre. And finally, he adds 2 or 3 swirls of uncle Giovanni's homemade red-wine vinegar. Dad tosses the salad quickly but gently, tastes it and nearly always adds a little more salt. With a pair of metal tongs and the bowl cradled above his hip, he then serves the salad, and always to the children first.

My favourite ingredient in Dad's salad is the rocket which he grows from seed. His rocket has the distinctive peppery, nutty, pungent flavour and is terrific in spring and autumn salads.

The sweet and sour of the Chicken Liver, Orange, Rocket and Pomegranate Salad on page 12 brings back memories of summer days sitting under our grapevine-covered loggia with my grandfather Gaetano. Nonno would cut orange and lemon segments, sprinkle them with a little salt, and then dip each citrus piece into a bowl of olive oil and home-made red-wine vinegar.

COS LETTUCE

PANZANELLA

CAPERS ADDED TO PANZANELLA GIVE IT A FRESH, DELICIOUS FLAVOUR

ROCKET FOR THE CHICKEN LIVER, ORANGE, ROCKET AND POMEGRANATE SALAD

DIEGO'S MIXED GREEN SALAD

1 cos lettuce
1 red oak lettuce
1 Italian oak lettuce
50 g baby spinach leaves
1 bunch rocket
4 inner stalks celery, leaves included
4 spring onions
1 bunch radish
1 Lebanese cucumber
150 g small black olives
1 punnet cherry tomatoes, halved
1 sprig fresh oregano, leaves only
salt and freshly ground pepper
dressing
6 tablespoons olive oil
2 tablespoons red-wine vinegar

Serves 12

1 Remove and discard all the outer leaves from the cos, red and Italian oak lettuces. Separate all 3 and soak in 2 or 3 changes of water.
2 The lettuce leaves must be thoroughly dry for the salad. I find the best way to do this is to place all the salad leaves in the centre of a large tea towel or small tablecloth, then gather up the corners in your hand making sure there are no gaps where you can see any leaves. Now swing your arm around in circles a few times to release the water.
3 Break up all the leaves into bite-size pieces by tearing down along the side of the inner stems and discard the stems. The small inner, tender leaves can be left whole. Place them all into a large serving bowl.
4 Trim the stems from spinach and rocket leaves. Soak in water and proceed as in steps 2 and 3. Add to the bowl with the other salad leaves.
5 Wash and dry the celery and spring onions. Finely slice them diagonally and add to the bowl.
6 Wash and dry the radish then trim the stalks, leaving about 2 cm of stem. Cut into 4 lengthwise and add to the bowl.
7 Wash and trim the cucumber. Halve lengthwise and cut diagonally into about 5 mm-thick slices. Add to the bowl.
8 Add the olives, tomatoes and oregano.
9 Season with salt and a little pepper.
10 Pour over the oil and then the red-wine vinegar and mix through gently to coat all the leaves well. Taste and adjust the seasoning before serving.

To serve: This is a big bowl of salad and you can reduce the amount of ingredients to suit your needs. Remember to not use too much oil as the leaves should never be soggy—just use enough oil to give them a little sheen. Also, be light-handed with the vinegar—you just need a hint to remind you it's there. Let everyone help themselves.

The salad should be prepared as close as possible to being served. To keep it crisp up until that time, place all the washed and dried cos, red and Italian oak leaves, spinach and rocket in a freezer bag and place in the fridge, ready to be taken out just before dressing. Leave the celery, onions, radish and cucumber whole but cleaned (ready to be cut later) and put each of these in separate bags in the fridge. Have the oil and vinegar ready.

PANZANELLA

2 small, long ciabatta rolls halved or 6 slices of ciabatta bread, 1 day old
2 red peppers, seeded, cut into wide strips lengthwise
2 tablespoons olive oil
salt and freshly ground pepper
2 medium ripe tomatoes, skinned
1 large Lebanese cucumber
80 g anchovy fillets, strained of oil
1 tablespoon capers, rinsed
1 small red onion, finely sliced

dressing
1 tablespoon virgin olive oil
1 teaspoon red-wine vinegar
1 clove garlic, finely chopped
salt and freshly ground pepper

Serves 6

1 Brush both sides of the ciabatta rolls or bread and the slices of red pepper with the oil. Season with salt and pepper.
2 Preheat the chargrill. Brush the grill with oil then grill the bread and the peppers.
3 Take off the heat and cut both the bread and peppers into bite-size pieces. Place the bread into a large serving bowl or shallow dish. Set the peppers aside.
4 Squeeze the tomatoes over the bowl so that the bread is covered with the tomato seeds and juice.
5 Chop the tomatoes and add to the bowl.
6 Cut cucumber into 4 lengthwise and cut into 1 cm slices and add to the salad.
7 Add the peppers, anchovies, capers and red onion.
8 Combine the dressing ingredients and pour over the salad.

To serve: You may serve this salad in a large bowl and let your guests help themselves or divide it up onto the centre of 6 plates.

LENTIL SALAD

3 tablespoons olive oil
1 shallot, finely chopped
300 g lentils, soaked overnight
¾ cup hot chicken stock or water
1 carrot, finely diced
2 celery stalks, peeled, finely diced
1 spring onion, sliced finely diagonally
3 small, hot red chillies, seeded and finely chopped
2 tablespoons flat-leaf parsley
1 handful fresh chervil leaves

dressing
3 tablespoons olive oil
juice ½ lemon
salt and freshly ground pepper

Serves 6

1 Heat the oil in a heavy-based saucepan. Add the shallot and cook until translucent.
2 Drain and wash the lentils and add to the saucepan with the shallot.
3 Stir and gently cook the lentils for 2 minutes. Add the stock or water and simmer until it is absorbed by the lentils.
4 Take off the heat and cool.
5 Place the lentils in a shallow dish and add the carrot, celery, spring onion, chillies, parsley and chervil.
6 Combine the dressing ingredients and pour over the salad. Stir thoroughly to mix well.

To serve: You may serve this salad in a serving bowl and let your guests help themselves or divide it onto 6 plates. Serve with grilled thick slices of sourdough bread that has been brushed with olive oil.

EGGPLANT AND GREEN BEAN SALAD

200 g green string beans, trim tops only
1 eggplant (about 350 g)
1 leek, white part only, cut into 7 mm discs
1 tablespoon capers, rinsed
50 g roasted pine nuts
2 tablespoons flat-leaf parsley, finely chopped
16 large black olives
16 cherry tomatoes
dressing
1 clove garlic, finely chopped
3 tablespoons olive oil
juice ½ lemon
½ teaspoon red-wine vinegar
salt and freshly ground pepper

Serves 4

1 Cook the beans in boiling water for 3 minutes and then refresh under cold running water. Set aside.
2 Cut eggplant into 1 cm discs. Salt both sides and place on absorbent paper. Leave for about 15 minutes.
3 Preheat the chargrill. Brush the grill with oil.
4 Brush the eggplant and leek with oil and grill until they are cooked.
5 Place the eggplant, leek, beans, capers, pine nuts, parsley, olives and tomatoes in a bowl.
6 Combine the dressing ingredients then pour over the salad and gently toss to mix well.

To serve: Divide the eggplant and leek onto the centre of 4 plates then top with the beans. Place the olives and cherry tomatoes around the edge then pour over what's left of the ingredients and serve.

CHICKEN LIVER, ORANGE, ROCKET AND POMEGRANATE SALAD

400 g chicken livers
2 tablespoons olive oil
½ small onion, finely sliced
3 tablespoons dry marsala or dry vermouth
salt and freshly ground pepper
100 g rocket
1 inner stalk celery, leaves included, finely sliced
1 orange
1 small pomegranate
1 tablespoon olive oil

Serves 4

1 Clean and trim the chicken livers especially any that may have a small green sack.
2 Heat the oil in a frying pan and add the onion and cook on a low heat for about 4 minutes until they start to go brown.
3 Add the chicken livers to the onion, turn up the heat to medium and cook for another 5 minutes until they start to go brown on the outside and are pink inside.
4 Add the marsala and cook for a further 2 minutes. Season with salt and pepper and set aside and keep warm.
5 Wash and dry the rocket and place in a serving bowl.
6 Add the celery.
7 Peel the orange and cut into segments. Add to the rocket and celery.
8 To peel the pomegranate, make a deep cut around the crown or blossom end and discard it. Score the skin into 4 vertically and with your thumbs inside the crown end, gently open the fruit. Pull away the rind and gently break off the seeds and set these aside.

To serve: Pour the oil over the rocket, celery and orange and season with salt and pepper. Divide this onto 4 plates. To the side of the rocket divide chicken livers and sprinkle the pomegranate seeds over the lot.

SALAD OF PARSLEY-CRUMBED BABY VEGETABLES

4 small female zucchini (with flowers attached)
2 baby fennel bulbs, washed and trimmed
2 baby cauliflowers, washed and trimmed of leaves
2 baby carrots, washed and trimmed

breadcrumb mixture
1 cup fine breadcrumbs
2 tablespoons flat-leaf parsley, finely chopped
¼ teaspoon garlic, finely chopped
3 eggs, lightly beaten
salt and freshly ground pepper
1½ cups olive oil

tomatoes
3 ripe tomatoes, skins removed
1 small clove garlic, chopped
1 cup (loosely-packed) flat-leaf parsley, chopped
1 cup (loosely-packed) basil leaves, chopped
2 tablespoons olive oil
salt and freshly ground pepper

Serves 4

1 Detach the flowers from the zucchini by holding on to the base of the flower and snapping to one side.
2 Gently wipe any grit or dirt from the flowers and trim the ends of the zucchini.
3 Cook all the vegetables (except the flowers) separately in boiling salted water until tender. (They should all take about about 5 minutes, with the zucchini taking 3 minutes.) Refresh under cold running water and set aside on absorbent paper.
4 While carrots are under the water, remove skin by rubbing it off, it will come off easily. Set aside.
5 Halve all the vegetables (except the zucchini and their flowers) lengthwise then set aside.
6 Combine all the breadcrumb mixture in a bowl except the eggs and oil and season with salt and pepper.
7 Dip all the vegetables (in batches) into the egg, then the breadcrumb mixture, and set aside on a tray ready for frying.
8 Heat the oil in a frying pan and gently fry all the vegetables so that they are golden brown on all sides. Set aside on absorbent paper.
9 Chop the tomatoes into small cubes and set aside in a bowl.
10 Pound the garlic, parsley and basil in a mortar until they form a paste. Add the oil and stir to mix well.
11 Add the parsley and basil mixture to the tomatoes and stir through to mix well. Season with salt and pepper.

To serve: Arrange the vegetables in the centre of 4 plates and spoon a little of the tomato mixture around them.

VEGETABLES

My mother-in-law Palmina always prepared big, red fleshy peppers by throwing them straight onto hot coals. On a sheet of corrugated iron in a cleared area of the backyard vegetable patch she would light a fire heaped with plenty of wood and dry cuttings from her husband's fruit trees. I loved watching her quietly sitting there on an old box, holding a piece of cardboard and waving her hand over the embers, fanning them to produce more heat. Once the fire had died down she would place the peppers in amongst the coals and poke them with a stick to make sure they were well covered. When the peppers were quite black, she would remove them from the coals and place them in the front pocket of her apron. While they were still warm and through the material of the apron, she would then rub the black skin off the peppers, pull off the stalks and break them in half to remove the seeds. Then she would tear them into strips and place them in a bowl, finishing with some olive oil and seasoning with salt and lots of freshly ground pepper.

In summer I cook whole eggplants and tomatoes like Palmina did in her backyard (see Palmina's Charcoal Eggplants and Tomatoes on page 20). In Sicily the popularity of the eggplant flourishes with dishes such as Caponata (sweet and sour eggplant), Melanzane Fritte (fried eggplant) and Melanzane alla Parmigiana (eggplant with cheese and a tomato sauce). My mother's mother, Rosa, would always prepare a breakfast of Melanzane alla Parmigiana when people came to buy goats from my grandfather Franco.

Eggplants are one of my favourite vegetables. If I were stranded on a desert island I would be quite happy with some eggplants and artichokes and the company of a few chickens so I could cook Pina's (my mother) Artichoke Frittata on page 32 with their eggs.

SWISS BROWN MUSHROOMS,
ZUCCHINI AND TOMATOES
READY TO BE CHARGRILLED

POTATOES STRAIGHT FROM THE GARDEN

ASPARAGUS

ARTICHOKES GROWING IN MY

FATHER'S GARDEN

PALMINA'S CHARCOAL EGGPLANTS AND TOMATOES

4 medium eggplants
8 ripe roma tomatoes
dressing
120 ml olive oil
1 clove garlic, peeled and finely chopped
1 handful tiny, whole basil leaves
salt and freshly ground pepper

Serves 4

1 Prepare a fire and burn enough wood to provide an ample amount of charcoal.
2 Place the eggplants and tomatoes straight onto the coals. Fan the coals occasionally to create more heat.
3 As the skins of the eggplants and tomatoes start to char and blister, turn them gently. Continue this process until the skins are scorched and evenly cooked all over.
4 Remove from the coals and place in a large dish to cool a little.
5 Meanwhile, combine all the dressing ingredients in a small bowl. Mix with a fork and set aside.
6 Peel the tomatoes and the eggplants, leaving the stems intact.

To serve: Arrange the eggplants and tomatoes on a serving dish. Pour the dressing over the top and serve with thick slices of crusty Italian-style bread.

PENNE WITH EGGPLANT, SPINACH AND TOMATO

8 Lebanese eggplants

400 g penne

1 bunch spinach, washed and stems removed

6 tablespoons olive oil

1 clove garlic, finely chopped

2 small hot red chillies, seeds removed and finely chopped

1 punnet cherry tomatoes, halved

3 tablespoons flat-leaf parsley, chopped

Serves 4

1 Cut eggplants in 4 lengthways. Salt cut side only and set aside for 30 minutes. When ready to cook eggplants, pat dry with absorbent paper and brush with oil.

2 Preheat the chargrill until very hot, then brush with oil and grill the eggplants on all sides. Cook for about 5 minutes on each side or until golden brown. Remove from the heat and set aside.

3 Meanwhile, bring water to the boil in a large saucepan then add salt and cook the pasta until just before *al dente*. You will have to act quickly here and add the spinach while the pasta is still in the water and stir through rapidly as it will wilt straightaway. Leave for about 1 minute.

4 Drain the lot. While this is draining return the same saucepan to the stove and add the oil, garlic and chillies, and cook gently for 30 seconds or until the garlic turns white. Add the tomatoes and stir to coat them well with the oil, garlic and chillies. Take off the heat then add the parsley and the pasta and the spinach and stir well.

To serve: Divide the pasta onto 4 plates and top with the grilled eggplant.

GRILLED VEGETABLES ON ROCKET AND RICOTTA

100 g rocket
200 g ricotta
25 g enoki mushrooms*
8 small to medium Swiss brown mushrooms
4 medium, ripe tomatoes, halved
1 zucchini, trimmed, cut diagonally into 8 slices
2 tablespoons olive oil
salt and freshly ground pepper

breadcrumbs
1 tablespoon olive oil
1 clove garlic, finely chopped
1 cup white breadcrumbs
2 tablespoons flat-leaf parsley, finely chopped
salt and freshly ground pepper

dressing
2 tablespoons olive oil
juice ½ lemon

Serves 4

1 Wash rocket and pat dry on absorbent paper. Arrange on a large white platter.
2 Break up the ricotta with your hands and place over the rocket leaves. Set the platter aside.
3 Trim the ends of the enoki mushrooms, rinse briefly under cold running water then pat dry thoroughly on absorbent paper and set aside.
4 Trim the ends of the Swiss brown mushrooms and wipe clean with damp absorbent paper. Brush the mushrooms, tomatoes and zucchini slices all over with 2 tablespoons of olive oil. Season with salt and pepper and set aside.
5 Heat 1 tablespoon of olive oil in a frying pan. Add the garlic and cook on a low heat for 30 seconds or until it turns white. Add the breadcrumbs and parsley and cook until the breadcrumbs are golden brown. Season with salt and pepper.
6 Preheat the chargrill. Brush the grill with oil and grill the Swiss brown mushrooms, tomatoes and zucchini slices on both sides, brushing with a little oil as you turn. Take off the heat.

To serve: Pour the dressing over the rocket and ricotta. Arrange the tomatoes (cut-side up) over the top. Place a Swiss brown mushroom (stem-side up) on each of the tomatoes and then spoon the breadcrumb mixture over the top. Cover with a zucchini slice and top each of the stacks with the enoki mushrooms.

*Enoki mushrooms have a lovely mild, earthy flavour. They are white with long, thin stems and tiny caps.

GRILLED ZUCCHINI AND GOAT'S CHEESE ON BARBECUED BREAD

4 small zucchini, halved lengthwise
4 thick slices of crusty Italian-style bread, halved lengthwise
2 tablespoons olive oil
1 clove garlic, peeled and halved
4 round slices fresh goat's cheese (from a log)
dressing
2 tablespoons olive oil
2 sprigs oregano, leaves only

Serves 4

1 Salt the zucchini on the cut side and set aside for 15 minutes.
2 Wipe off the zucchini juice with absorbent paper.
3 Brush the zucchini and the bread with the oil.
4 Preheat the chargrill. Brush the grill with oil and grill the zucchini and the bread until golden brown.
5 Take off the heat and rub the bread on both sides with the cut garlic.

To serve: In the centre of 4 plates, place one half of each slice of bread and rest the other slice to one side. Crisscross 2 zucchini halves cut-side up over the bread. Pour some of the dressing over the zucchini, arrange a slice of the goat's cheese and then pour over the remaining dressing.

ASPARAGUS AND LONG GREEN PEPPERS

600 g asparagus (of the same thickness)
4 long green peppers
2 tablespoons olive oil
salt and freshly ground pepper
125 g pine nuts, browned in oven
parmesan shavings

Serves 4

1 Trim asparagus to the same length as the peppers, then cook in boiling water for 1 minute and drain and set aside.
2 Cut the peppers into 4 lengthwise and scoop out the seeds.
3 Brush the asparagus and peppers with the oil and season with salt and pepper.
4 Preheat the chargrill. Brush the grill with oil and grill the asparagus and peppers, brushing with a little oil while they are cooking.

To serve: Arrange the asparagus and peppers on a shallow dish all facing the same direction. Sprinkle with the pine nuts and top with shavings of the cheese.

STUFFED LONG GREEN PEPPERS

8 long green peppers
stuffing
2 ripe tomatoes, skin and seeds removed, finely chopped
2 cups breadcrumbs
45 g anchovies, finely chopped
1 tablespoon fresh oregano, finely chopped
3 tablespoons olive oil
salt and freshly ground pepper
salad
50 g mixed salad leaves
1 tablespoon olive oil
¼ teaspoon balsamic vinegar
salt and freshly ground pepper

Serves 4

1 Cut around the stem of each pepper and gently pull it out. Tap the peppers on all sides against the bench and shake to release most of the seeds. Set aside.
2 Combine all of the stuffing ingredients in a bowl and mix well with your hands.
3 Stuff each of the peppers with the breadcrumb mixture. Press the mixture down firmly using your thumb as you stuff each pepper. Brush the peppers with a little oil.
4 Preheat the chargrill. Brush the grill with oil.
5 Grill the peppers until they are cooked then set aside.

To serve: Divide the mixed salad leaves onto the centre of 4 plates. On either side of this, place 2 peppers facing in opposite directions. Pour the oil and then the vinegar over the salad leaves and a little over the peppers. Season the leaves with salt and pepper.

PINA'S ARTICHOKE FRITTATA

4 fresh medium artichokes
½ lemon
4 tablespoons olive oil
1 tablespoon onion, finely chopped
4 eggs
salt and freshly ground pepper

Serves 4

1 Cut the stems off the artichokes and remove the outer leaves until you are left with the tender inner leaves only. Trim around the edge.
2 Cut 2.5 cm from the tops to remove the darker, spiky tipped portion of the leaves. As you work, rub all over the cut surfaces with lemon to stop them from discolouring.
3 Halve the artichokes lengthwise and then cut each half into 4.
4 Place the artichokes into a saucepan of boiling water and cook for about 5–7 minutes or until tender. Drain and set aside.
5 Heat the oil in a non-stick frying pan. Add the onion and artichokes and cook gently for about 7 minutes until the edges of the artichokes begin to go golden brown and crispy.
6 Add the eggs, cracking them one at a time over the artichokes and onion. Season with salt and pepper.
7 Break the yolks with a wooden spoon or spatula, stirring the eggs into the artichokes and onion. Cook until the bottom of the frittata is a golden colour.
8 Break up the frittata into 4 using the side of the spatula and flip to cook the other side until lightly golden.

To serve: Place the frittata onto a serving dish for everyone to help themselves. Serve with a green leaf salad and thick slices of crusty Italian-style bread.

CAVULISCEDDI AND GOAT'S CHEESE FRITTATA

3 tablespoons olive oil
200 g cavulisceddi* (leaves only), washed
salt and freshly ground pepper
5 eggs
2 tablespoons parmesan, freshly grated
1 spring onion, finely sliced diagonally
100 g soft goat's cheese

Serves 4

1 Heat the oil in a frying pan.
2 Add the cavulisceddi then cover and cook on a medium heat for about 2–3 minutes.
3 Meanwhile, break all of the eggs into a bowl and stir briskly with a fork to mix well.
4 Add the parmesan, season with salt and pepper and stir to mix well. Set aside.
5 Pour the eggs into the frying pan over the cavulisceddi.
6 Add the spring onion evenly over the top of the frittata.
7 Crumble the goat's cheese with your fingers over the top of the frittata and cook on a medium heat until the bottom of the frittata is golden.
8 Cook the top under a grill or place in a hot oven for about 5 minutes until lightly golden.

To serve: Slide the frittata onto a serving dish and cut into 4 at the table. Let everyone help themselves and serve with fresh crusty Italian-style bread.

* Cavulisceddi leaves have a similar flavour to tender young, fresh radish leaves. My father grows them from seeds so they are ready to eat at the beginning of autumn. Mum cooks the stems and leaves in a little olive oil with garlic and tomatoes until they become golden brown and crunchy and they are delicious with fresh crusty Italian-style bread. Cavulisceddi can be purchased from Italian greengrocers or better still, grow your own. The seeds can be bought from a good Italian deli. If you can't get any cavulisceddi, substitute rapuddi or rapi (rape) or young wild rocket leaves or very tender, young fresh radish leaves.

MEAT

In the middle of our backyard there is a bare stretch of lawn. At either end are patches where bowlers and batsmen have fought many battles. As a long-suffering fieldsman and father of three, my position is usually at silly mid-off or mid-wicket. Sometimes I am moved to fly slip by my captain, but my favourite position of all is at deep backward square leg. In the late afternoon warmth I stand, forgotten, dreaming of flames and embers, marinades and sauces, and of beef, lamb and pork grilling over hot coals.

In this daydream I cook on 'the backyard monument', a barbecue built with my own hands. I have always dreamt of designing and building my own barbecue in amongst the roses and lavender bushes with a stepping-stone path leading up to it. This dream is inspired by my father who has a barbecue surrounded by fig and apricot trees built into his gravel courtyard.

Just before I start chargrilling meat I lightly brush the grill with oil or with a piece of fat trimmed from the meat. If you are cooking on a barbecue, you can throw some rosemary branches or twigs from fruit trees onto the fire which will give your food a fragrant flavour. A terrific way of basting meat while it is cooking is with a herb brush. The flavours of the Eye Fillet with Tomato, Oregano and Boiled Potatoes (see page 47) are enhanced by basting with a brush made from fresh 20 cm-long oregano sprigs tied at one end with kitchen string.

An important part of cooking poultry and red meat is the concept of resting the food after cooking. By resting the meat for the same amount of time as it took to cook or for at least 10 minutes before serving, you retain the maximum amount of juices and allow the meat to relax.

A RACK OF LAMB ON THE CHARGRILL

AN EYE FILLET BEING BRUSHED WITH OREGANO

PORTERHOUSE STEAK MARINATING IN A MIXTURE OF HERBS AND SPICES

ITALIAN SAUSAGES WITH MIXED HERBS

RACK OF LAMB WITH EGGPLANTS AND ROSEMARY WALNUT PESTO

6 Lebanese eggplants
salt
4 racks of lamb (4 cutlets on each rack)

marinade
½ cup olive oil
2 cloves garlic, finely chopped
½ cup rosemary, leaves only
salt and freshly ground pepper

rosemary walnut pesto
1 clove garlic, roughly sliced
50 g walnuts, roughly chopped
¼ cup rosemary, leaves only
½ cup flat-leaf parsley, leaves only, finely chopped
½ cup olive oil
freshly ground pepper

Serves 4

1 Cut eggplants in half lengthways. Salt cut side only and set aside for 1 hour.
2 Cut away the outer bones of the lamb leaving 2 middle bones only. Trim of all fat.
3 Place lamb racks on a shallow dish and cover with the oil, garlic and rosemary. Season with salt and lots of pepper. Marinate for 1 hour at room temperature or overnight in the fridge (but bring back to room temperature before cooking).
4 Preheat the chargrill. Brush the grill with oil and cook the lamb racks for 8–10 minutes on each side or until cooked to your liking. Brush the lamb with the marinade as it is cooking.
5 Take the lamb off the heat, wrap in foil and set aside for 20 minutes.
6 Wash and pat dry the eggplant with absorbent paper and brush with leftover marinade mixture from the lamb racks. Chargrill until golden brown—about 5 minutes on the cut side and 2–3 minutes on the other side. Place on absorbent paper and set aside.
7 Combine the garlic, walnuts, rosemary, parsley and oil in a blender to make pesto. Blend until well pureed then add pepper.

To serve: Place a rack of lamb in the centre of 4 plates and arrange 2 eggplant halves to one side of the lamb. Spoon pesto over lamb and serve.

LAMB CUTLETS WITH BROAD BEANS AND POTATO PATTIES

12 lamb cutlets
2 tablespoons olive oil
salt and freshly ground pepper

broad beans
2 kg broad beans, twice peeled
1 tablespoon olive oil
25 g butter
1 shallot, finely chopped
1 tablespoon wild fennel or dill, finely chopped

potato patties
500 g desiree potatoes, boiled and peeled
¼ cup parmesan
1 tablespoon flat-leaf parsley, finely chopped
1 small clove garlic, finely chopped
1 egg
salt and freshly ground pepper
3 tablespoons olive oil

Serves 4

1 Trim lamb cutlets of all fat and brush with the oil. Season with salt and pepper and set aside.
2 To prepare the broad beans, heat the oil and butter in a frying pan, then add the shallot and gently cook until translucent.
3 Add the broad beans, then stir and cook for 2 minutes. Add enough water (about ¾ cup) to just cover the broad beans and gently cook for about another 10 minutes. Take off the heat and add the wild fennel or dill. Set aside and keep warm.
4 Place the potatoes in a bowl and mash.
5 Add the parmesan, parsley, garlic and egg. Season with salt and pepper and stir well. (This mixture will make 4 potato patties.)
6 Lightly brush 4 egg rings with oil and divide the potato mixture into these, flattening and shaping the patties with the palms of your hands. Take out of the moulds and set aside on a plate.
7 Heat the oil in a frying pan and on a medium heat, cook the patties until golden brown. Place on absorbent paper towels to absorb all the oil and set aside and keep warm.
8 Preheat the chargrill. Brush the grill with oil and cook the lamb cutlets for about 3–5 minutes on each side or to your liking.
9 Take off the heat, set aside and keep warm for 10 minutes.

To serve: Have 4 warm plates ready. Spoon the broad-bean mixture onto the centre of each plate and place a potato pattie over the top. Arrange the lamb cutlets over the patties and serve.

ROSEMARY AND GARLIC-STUFFED LAMB WITH SPINACH AND RED PEPPER SAUCE

2 boned loins of lamb (about 600 g each)

stuffing

2 tablespoons olive oil

2 cloves garlic, finely chopped

salt and freshly ground pepper

½ bunch or 12 sprigs rosemary

spinach

1 bunch spinach

salt and freshly ground pepper

1 tablespoon olive oil

red pepper sauce

3 tablespoons olive oil

1 small onion, finely chopped

½ kg ripe roma tomatoes, roughly chopped

6 basil leaves

2 red peppers (about 300 g each)

salt and freshly ground pepper

Serves 4

1 Trim top layer of skin (still leaving some fat) from each of the boned loins.

2 For the stuffing, combine oil and garlic and brush all over the meat. Season with salt and pepper.

3 Place the rosemary in the centre of each loin. With the thinnest part of the loin towards you, roll the meat away from you very tightly. Halve each loin and tie in the middle with wet kitchen string.

4 Trim each side of the lamb, cutting away any of the rosemary leaves and set aside.

5 Remove the stems from the spinach.

6 To wash the leaves, fill the basin in the kitchen sink with water and soak the spinach for about 10 minutes. Remove from the water. Change the water and repeat twice more until there is no trace of grit in the water then set aside.

7 For the red pepper sauce, heat the oil in a pan and gently fry the onion until translucent. Add the tomatoes and cook for another 15 minutes.

8 Remove tomato sauce from the pan and press through a Mouli using the disc with the small holes. (A Mouli is a food mill for processing tomatoes, ricotta, potatoes etc. If you don't have one, press the sauce through a sieve and discard the seeds and skin.) Add the basil to the sauce and set aside.

9 Preheat the chargrill. Brush the grill and the peppers with oil and grill until the skins begin to turn black and blister. Set aside to cool.

10 Peel the skin from the peppers, remove the seeds, then cut into strips.

11 Remove the basil leaves from the tomato sauce and discard.

12 Pour the tomato sauce and add the sliced peppers into a food processor. Season with salt and pepper and puree the mixture. Set aside and keep warm.

13 Preheat the hot plate on the barbecue or chargrill, then turn down the heat and gently cook the stuffed loins. Cook for about 15–20 minutes or to your liking. Set aside for 15 minutes and keep warm.

14 Add the spinach and any water that has drained to the bottom of the bowl to a large pot or wok. Cover and cook until spinach starts to wilt. Drain and place into a bowl, season with salt and pepper and pour the oil over the top.

To serve: Pour a little of the red pepper sauce in the centre of 4 warm plates. Place the spinach on top of the sauce. Remove the string from the loins and arrange them on top of the spinach.

EYE FILLET WITH TOMATO, OREGANO AND BOILED POTATOES

650 g eye fillet (in one piece)
small bunch oregano, tied together at the stems

stuffing

1 clove garlic
½ cup basil leaves
¼ teaspoon salt
1 kg ripe tomatoes, skin and seeds removed, coarsely chopped
½ cup oregano leaves
½ cup olive oil
salt and freshly ground pepper
2 tablespoons parmesan cheese, grated

potatoes

4 medium desiree potatoes, washed and unpeeled
2 tablespoons olive oil
salt and freshly ground pepper

Serves 4

1 Make a cutting lengthwise halfway into the fillet and set aside.
2 Pound the garlic and basil leaves in a mortar with the salt until it forms a paste. (If you don't have a mortar just chop the garlic and basil finely.) Transfer to a bowl and add the tomatoes, oregano and oil. Season with salt and pepper and stir well.
3 Fold away the sides of the fillet and spoon some of the tomato mixture into the cut. Sprinkle with the cheese and season with salt and pepper.
4 Close up the fillet and tie with kitchen string and season the outside. Place into a shallow dish and cover with the rest of the tomato mixture and marinate for 1 hour at room temperature. (You can also marinate overnight in the fridge but bring back to room temperature before cooking.)
5 Preheat the chargrill. Brush the grill with oil then grill the fillet, basting with the tomato mixture using the oregano brush. The fillet should take 25–30 minutes or cook to your liking. Wrap the fillet in foil and set aside for 30 minutes. Set the tomato mixture aside also.
6 Cook the potatoes in boiling salted water until tender. Drain and cut into quarters. Return to the saucepan and pour over the oil. Season with salt and lots of freshly ground pepper and stir gently to cover the potatoes well.

To serve: Place 4 quarters of potato on each plate. Spoon a little of the oil over each. Remove string from the fillet and cut into 4. Place each slice of meat in the centre of each plate then spoon over the tomato mixture and serve.

MUSTARD MARINATED STEAK WITH RED AND YELLOW PEPPERS

1 kg scotch fillet, cut into 12 thin slices

marinade

3 tablespoons Dijon seed mustard

1 clove garlic, finely chopped

2 tablespoons olive oil

3 sprigs rosemary, leaves only

salt and freshly ground pepper

peppers

2 red peppers

2 yellow peppers

4 tablespoons olive oil

juice 1 lime

2 sprigs oregano, leaves only

salt and freshly ground pepper

Serves 6

1 Combine all the marinade ingredients and brush all over the meat. Marinate for 1 hour.

2 Cut the peppers lengthwise into strips.

3 Place the peppers in a shallow dish and add the oil, lime juice, oregano and salt and pepper.

4 Preheat the chargrill. Brush the grill with oil.

5 Grill the steaks for about 2 minutes on each side or until meat is cooked to your liking, brushing lightly with the marinade while cooking. Set aside for 10 minutes and keep warm.

6 Grill the peppers until they are cooked and set aside ready to serve.

To serve: Place the steaks in the centre of 6 warm plates and top with a mixture of the red and yellow peppers. Serve with thick slices of lightly oiled grilled sourdough bread.

PORTERHOUSE STEAK WITH MUSHROOMS

2 kg porterhouse or strip loin (in one piece)

marinade

1 teaspoon whole coriander seeds

1 teaspoon whole cumin seeds

1 clove garlic, crushed

1 small hot red chilli, seeds removed and finely chopped

2 tablespoons flat-leaf parsley, finely chopped

2 tablespoons coriander, finely chopped

6 tablespoons olive oil

salt and freshly ground pepper

mushrooms

350 g small whole mushrooms

1 leek

4 tablespoons olive oil

1 tablespoon tomato paste

1 cup chicken stock or water

1 tablespoon flat-leaf parsley, finely chopped

salt and freshly ground pepper

Serves 4

1 Trim the porterhouse of all fat and cut into 4 steaks.

2 Pound the steaks lightly and place them in a large shallow dish.

3 Pound the coriander and cumin seeds in a mortar then combine with the rest of the marinade ingredients and pour over the steaks to coat well. Marinate overnight or for at least 3 hours.

4 Clean the mushrooms, wiping them with damp absorbent paper then set aside.

5 Cut the white part of the leek into 5 mm-wide slices and set aside.

6 Heat the oil in a saucepan then add the mushrooms and leek, stirring to coat well with the oil. Cover and cook on a low heat for about 5 minutes, stirring occasionally.

7 Add the tomato paste and stock or water and cook uncovered for another 15 minutes on medium heat or until liquid has reduced by half. Add parsley and season with salt and pepper. Set aside and keep warm.

8 Preheat the chargrill then brush the grill with oil. On a medium heat, grill the meat for about 5–6 minutes on each side (or to your taste), brushing the cooked side with the marinade mixture. Take off the heat and place back into the dish with the marinade. Keep warm and rest for about 15 minutes.

To serve: Place the steaks in the centre of 4 warm plates and spoon over the mushrooms.

ITALIAN SAUSAGES WITH APPLES AND HAZELNUTS

8 Italian pork sausages
2 tablespoons olive oil
salt and freshly ground pepper
4 medium-large Granny Smith apples
3 tablespoons grapeseed oil
½ teaspoon garam masala
1 teaspoon balsamic vinegar
75 g roasted hazelnuts, roughly chopped

Serves 4

1 Cut the sausages and remove the string. Brush lightly with oil and season with salt and pepper.
2 Preheat the chargrill then brush the grill with oil. Grill the sausages and brush lightly with oil as you turn. Set aside and keep warm.
3 Quarter the apples and remove the cores. Peel and slice thinly lengthwise. Heat the grapeseed oil in a frying pan then add the apples, garam masala and balsamic vinegar and stir and cook on a medium heat until apples start to turn golden. Season apples with pepper.

To serve: Pile the apples in the centre of 4 plates. Sprinkle the hazelnuts over the top. Cut the sausages in half diagonally and place around the outside of the apples.

ITALIAN SAUSAGES WITH GARLIC AND ROSEMARY ROAST POTATOES

16 Italian pork sausages (left in one continous length)
3 tablespoons olive oil
3 tablespoon flat-leaf parsley, finely chopped
3 tablespoons mint, finely sliced
6 basil leaves, finely sliced
1 teaspoon of rosemary, finely chopped
salt and freshly ground pepper

potatoes
750 g desiree potatoes
1 head garlic, cloves separated
sprig rosemary, leaves only
4 tablespoons olive oil
salt and freshly ground pepper

Serves 8

1 Coil the uncut sausages into one tight continuous round.
2 Pierce 2 metal skewers at right angles through the sausage coil to hold it in place.
3 Brush both sides of the sausages with the oil then place the coil in a large shallow dish and sprinkle with all the herbs, making sure to rub all over and under the sausages. Season with salt and pepper.
4 Cut the potatoes into bite-size pieces and place in a baking tray. Add the garlic, rosemary and oil then season with salt and pepper and place in a preheated 180°C oven for 1–1¼ hours.
5 Preheat the chargrill then brush the grill with oil. Grill the sausages and brush with the herb and oil mixture as you turn. Set aside and keep warm.

To serve: Place the sausage coil on a large round platter. Remove the string and cut the links with kitchen scissors. Place all the potatoes in a serving bowl. Take both to the table and let everyone help themselves.

PORK FILLETS WITH ZUCCHINI AND CARROTS

2 pork fillets (about 375–400 g each)

marinade

1 medium onion, chopped

1 clove garlic, finely chopped

1 cup freshly squeezed orange juice

2 teaspoons caraway seeds

4 tablespoons olive oil

salt and freshly ground pepper

1 teaspoon cornflour, diluted in a little water

50 g butter

1 cup dry white wine

1 teaspoon balsamic vinegar

zucchini and carrots

2 medium-size zucchini

4 carrots, about 50 g each

salt and freshly ground pepper

Serves 4

1 Remove the sinew from the pork with a sharp knife. Cut both fillets in half diagonally and place in a shallow dish.

2 For the marinade, combine the onion, garlic, orange juice, caraway seeds and oil and season with salt and pepper.

3 Pour the marinade over the pork and marinate for about 1 hour.

4 Trim the zucchini, cut into 4 lengthwise and place on absorbent paper. Season with salt and set aside.

5 Wash and trim the carrots to the same length. Cook in boiling salted water for 3 minutes. Cut in half lengthwise, brush lightly with olive oil and season with salt and pepper.

6 Preheat the chargrill then brush the grill with oil. Grill the pork for about 8–10 minutes on each side, brushing with oil while it is cooking. Set aside the marinade mixture. Take the pork off the heat and keep warm for about 15 minutes.

7 Brush the zucchini lightly with oil and season with pepper.

8 Grill the zucchini and carrot slices then set aside and keep warm.

9 Melt the butter in a frying pan and add what is left of the marinade mixture. Cook this for about 1 minute then add the wine and vinegar. Simmer and let the liquid reduce by half. Add the cornflour and water and stir. As soon as it thickens a little, strain and keep warm.

To serve: Make a cross with the carrot halves in the centre of 4 plates. Place the zucchini slices over the carrots. Cut both of the pork fillets diagonally into 4 slices and place on top of the vegetables. Spoon a little of the marinade over each of the plates.

MARINATED PORK KEBABS WITH MANGO

12 wooden satay sticks
2 pork fillets, about 250 g each

marinade
1 garlic clove, finely chopped
1 tablespoon ginger, finely chopped
2 small hot red chillies, seeds removed and finely chopped
1 teaspoon rosemary, finely chopped
4 tablespoons extra light olive oil
salt and freshly ground black pepper

mangoes
3 large mangoes
juice 1 lime
freshly ground pepper

Serves 4

1 Soak the 12 wooden satay sticks in water for 1 hour.
2 Remove the sinew from the pork with a sharp knife.
3 Cut each fillet in half lengthwise then cut each half across the grain into bite-size pieces.
4 Combine the pork with the marinade ingredients in a shallow dish. Season with salt and pepper then marinate for 1 hour.
5 Preheat the chargrill then brush the grill with oil. Thread the pieces of pork evenly onto the sticks.
6 Grill the kebabs over a low heat until the meat is cooked to your liking, brushing lightly with the marinade while meat is cooking. Set aside for 15 minutes and keep warm.
7 Peel the mangoes and cut in half (as close to the stone as you can). Cut each half lengthwise into thin slices.
8 Place the mango slices in a bowl, add the lime juice and season with pepper. Stir gently to mix well.

To serve: Place 3 kebabs in the centre of each plate and spoon the mango to one side.

POULTRY

My father's mother, Giovanna-Giuseppina, had a large hillside plot near the village of Calatafimi, Sicily where she raised chooks. Here they roamed unrestrained and frenetic, gathering at her feet each day as she threw them kitchen scraps. She sold and bartered their eggs in the local piazza. On carnival days, feast days of saints and at Christmas and New Year Nonna would always cook 2 or 3 chicken dishes. My favourite was her light, honey-coloured chicken broth. Floating in this lustrous liquid would be rice or pastina and tiny chicken meatballs. Sometimes she would also put chicken feet into the broth and if she liked you, she would add 1 of these to your bowl.

The portions of chicken that Nonna and everybody loved the best were the stuffed necks. The necks with the head still attached would be stuffed with beadcrumbs, parsley, garlic and pecorino cheese and fried in the family's virgin olive oil. They were then placed into a saucepan of simmering tomato sauce. Nonna's stuffing for the necks is the inspiration for the Macadamia-Stuffed Chicken Drumsticks on page 68.

MACADAMIA-STUFFED
CHICKEN DRUMSTICKS

CHICKEN BURGER WITH
CHARGRILLED VEGETABLES

QUAILS READY TO BE CHARGRILLED

ROAST DUCK WITH CAVULISCEDDI
AND CARAMELISED APPLE

CHICKEN BREAST WITH RICOTTA AND SPINACH

4 chicken breasts, skin removed

marinade

zest 1 lemon, minced

2 tablespoons rosemary, leaves only, finely chopped

1 clove garlic, finely chopped

4 tablespoons olive oil

juice 1 lemon

salt and freshly ground pepper

ricotta

250 g ricotta

1 tablespoon pine nuts, lightly roasted

1 teaspoon lemon zest, minced

¼ teaspoon freshly grated nutmeg

2 teaspoons olive oil

½ teaspoon flat-leaf parsley, chopped

salt and freshly ground pepper

spinach

1 tablespoon olive oil

1 bunch spinach, washed, stems removed

salt and freshly ground pepper

Serves 4

1 Wash chicken breasts and pat dry with absorbent paper. Place the chicken breasts in a bowl.

2 Combine all the marinade ingredients and pour over the chicken, turning the breasts to coat thoroughly. Marinate for 15 minutes, turning the chicken occasionally.

3 Combine the ricotta, pine nuts, lemon zest, nutmeg, oil and parsley in a bowl and season with salt and pepper. Stir to mix through all the ingredients and set aside.

4 Preheat the chargrill then brush the grill with oil. Remove chicken from the marinade and cook over a low to medium heat for 5–7 minutes then lightly brush with oil and turn. Cook for another 5–7 minutes. Take off the heat, set aside and keep warm.

5 While the chicken is set aside, heat the oil in a frying pan or wok, add the spinach and cook until it has wilted. Season with salt and pepper.

6 While the spinach is cooking, heat the marinade mixture in a small saucepan. Cook this for about 1 minute.

To serve: Divide the spinach between 4 warm plates. Slice each of the chicken breasts diagonally into 4 and place on top of the spinach. Spoon the marinade mixture over the chicken and spinach and top each with a portion of ricotta shaped like a quenelle. (To shape the ricotta, fill a spoon with the ricotta mixture, dip another spoon into boiling water and invert over the spoon with ricotta mixture to mould into an oval shape. With the second spoon, gently ease the quenelle-shaped ricotta over the top of the chicken.)

CHICKEN BREAST WITH BASIL MAYONNAISE AND COS SALAD

4 chicken breasts, skin removed
2 tablespoons olive oil
salt and freshly ground pepper

mayonnaise
10 basil leaves, roughly torn
1 clove garlic, sliced
salt
1 egg yolk
¾ cup light olive oil
juice ½ small lemon
freshly ground pepper

salad
inner tender leaves cos lettuce
1 tablespoon olive oil
½ teaspoon balsamic vinegar
salt and freshly ground pepper

Serves 4

1 Wash chicken breasts and pat dry with absorbent paper. Place in a bowl and add the oil and season with salt and pepper, making sure to rub the oil and seasoning all over the chicken.
2 Make sure that the mayonnaise ingredients and both the bowls needed are at room temperature.
3 Combine the basil, garlic and a good pinch of salt in a mortar and pound well until it becomes a paste. (If you don't have a mortar just chop the garlic and basil finely.)
4 Spoon all of the mixture into a larger bowl then add the egg yolk and stir thoroughly with a wooden spoon or wire whisk until it has a smooth consistency. (Place a folded tea towel under the bowl to stop it from moving around too much.)
5 Add the oil, a drop at a time, ensuring that it is being absorbed completely. Once the mixture starts to thicken, the oil can be added in a slow, thin drizzle.
6 When a third of the oil has been combined, add the lemon juice a little at a time. Continue adding the rest of the oil until it is well incorporated then season with pepper and set aside.
7 Preheat the chargrill to a low to medium heat, brush with oil and cook the chicken breasts for 5–7 minutes then brush lightly with oil and turn. Cook for another 5–7 minutes then take off the heat and set aside to cool.

To serve: Cut the chicken breasts into diagonal pieces. Place into a bowl, add the basil mayonnaise and mix well. Place on a serving dish and take to the table. Put the cos leaves into a serving bowl then pour over the oil and vinegar. Season with salt and pepper and mix well.

MACADAMIA–STUFFED CHICKEN DRUMSTICKS

12 chicken drumsticks
stuffing
2 tablespoons olive oil
1 small onion, finely chopped
2 rashers rindless bacon, finely chopped
125 g macadamia nuts, chopped
1 tablespoon flat-leaf parsley, finely sliced
marinade
4 tablespoons olive oil
salt and freshly ground pepper
3 sprigs rosemary, leaves only

Serves 6

1 Wash the drumsticks, pat dry with absorbent paper and set aside.
2 To prepare the stuffing, heat the oil in a frying pan then add the onion and gently cook until translucent. Add the bacon and cook for a further 2 minutes. Add the chopped macadamia nuts and cook for another minute, stirring constantly. Take off the heat and stir through the parsley then set aside to cool.
3 To stuff the chicken, carefully loosen and pull back the skin from each drumstick. Make a cut lengthwise into each drumstick and spoon a little of the stuffing into the pocket. Press the sides of the pocket together with your fingers and pull back the skin firmly over the cut. Set aside in a flat dish.
4 Combine all of the marinade ingredients and brush each of the drumsticks to coat well. Leave to marinate for 1 hour.
5 Preheat the chargrill then brush the grill with oil. Cook the drumsticks for about 20–25 minutes, turning occasionally, until the chicken is cooked through. (Lightly brush the drumsticks with the marinade before turning each time.)

To serve: Pile drumsticks high on a large serving dish.

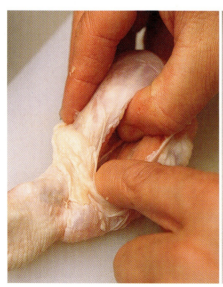 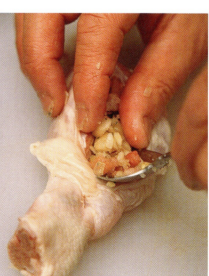 

CHICKEN THIGHS STUFFED WITH LIME AND BABY BEETS

4 chicken thighs
1 bunch baby beets (reserve leaves for stuffing)
3 tablespoons olive oil
salt and freshly ground pepper
½ lime, quartered

stuffing
1 lime (reserve juice for marinade)
1 lemon
1 bunch baby beet leaves only
4 sprigs basil
1 cm piece ginger, peeled and quartered

marinade
3 tablespoons olive oil
lime juice

Serves 4

1 Wash chicken thighs then pat dry with absorbent paper and set aside.
2 Remove outer leaves from the baby beets, washing and reserving 8 of the tender inner leaves for the stuffing.
3 Cook the baby beets in a pot of boiling water for about 10–15 minutes. Drain and dress with the oil and season with salt and pepper.
4 Peel 8 strips (as thin as possible) from both the lime and lemon using a vegetable peeler. Mince 4 of each of the strips and combine and set aside. Squeeze juice from the lime and set aside.
5 Turn the thighs so that the skin side is resting on the bench. Trim of any untidy bits then stuff the middle of each thigh with a sprig of basil, a slice of ginger, a lime and lemon strip and 2 baby beet leaves. Fold to cover the stuffing and tie in the middle with wet kitchen string.
6 Arrange chicken thighs in a shallow dish and sprinkle with the minced lime and lemon and season with salt and pepper. Pour over the olive oil and lime juice. Season with salt and pepper. Marinate for 1 hour at room temperature.
7 Preheat the chargrill. Brush the grill with oil and cook the chicken skin-side down on a very low heat, basting with the marinade mixture while it is cooking. Then cook the other side. (Each side should take about 15–20 minutes.) Wrap in foil and set aside for about 10–15 minutes.

To serve: Place a chicken thigh skin-side up in the centre of each plate with a wedge of lime and the baby beets to one side.

CHICKEN BURGERS WITH GRILLED VEGETABLES

1 kg chicken breasts, skin removed
1 tablespoon flat-leaf parsley, finely chopped
1 teaspoon rosemary, finely chopped
1 teaspoon sage, finely sliced
1 clove garlic, finely chopped
100 g dried apricots, finely chopped
50 g hazelnuts, roughly chopped
1 tablespoon freshly grated parmesan
2 eggs
2 tablespoons olive oil
60 g breadcrumbs
salt and freshly ground pepper

tomato and chilli sauce
2 tablespoons olive oil
2 tablespoons onion, finely chopped
2 small hot red chillies, seeds removed, finely chopped
1 clove garlic, finely chopped
500 g ripe tomatoes, skin and seeds removed, chopped
salt and freshly ground pepper
6 basil leaves

vegetables
250 g beetroot, washed and trimmed
1 tablespoon olive oil
dash balsamic vinegar
salt and freshly ground pepper
6 brussels sprouts
12 thick slices baguette
100 g rocket
2 yellow peppers, grilled, seeds removed and sliced
2 red peppers, grilled, seeds removed and sliced
12 slices zucchini, grilled
12 black olives

Serves 12

1 Chop the chicken breasts into chunks and mince in a food processor for about 10–15 seconds (do not blend them into a paste).
2 Combine the chicken, parsley, rosemary, sage, garlic, apricots, hazelnuts, parmesan, eggs, oil and breadcrumbs in a bowl. Season with salt and pepper.
3 Cover with cling wrap and refrigerate for about 1 hour.
4 To make the tomato and chilli sauce, heat the oil in a frying pan and gently fry the onion until translucent. Add the chillies and garlic and gently cook until the garlic turns white. Add the tomatoes and cook over a low heat for 15 minutes then season with salt and pepper. Take off the heat, add the basil leaves and keep warm.
5 Place the beetroot in a pot of boiling salted water and cook until just tender. Drain and place under cold running water to remove the skin.
6 Cut beetroot into 12 slices and place into a bowl. Dress with the oil and vinegar and season with salt and pepper and set aside.
7 Cook the brussels sprouts in boiling salted water for 3 minutes. Drain and refresh under cold running water. Halve lengthwise and dress with a little olive oil and season with freshly ground pepper. Set aside.
8 Form the chicken mixture into 12 burgers.
9 Preheat the chargrill then brush the grill with oil. Grill the chicken burgers over a low heat until meat is cooked, brushing lightly with oil while cooking. Set aside for 10–15 minutes and keep warm.
10 To finish the sauce, pour the tomato mixture into a blender and blend for about 5–10 seconds. Set aside and keep warm.
11 Lightly brush the bread with olive oil and grill both sides. Take off the heat.

To serve: Place the bread on a platter. On each slice pile up the following: rocket, red and yellow pepper strips, beetroot, chicken burger, zucchini slice. Spoon over a little of the sauce and then add the brussels sprout. Now to the tricky bit. Gently hold down each burger stack and pierce with a short wooden satay stick, down through the sprout and through to the bread. Now thread a black olive onto each stick so it sits on top of the burger.

ROAST CHICKEN WITH EGGPLANT, ZUCCHINI AND RED PEPPER

2 small (no. 11) free-range chickens
salt and freshly ground pepper
6 tablespoons olive oil
2 cloves garlic, crushed with back of knife

vegetables
350 g eggplant
salt
2 small green zucchini
2 small yellow zucchini
1 red pepper
6 tablespoons olive oil
1 small onion, finely chopped
1 clove garlic, crushed with back of knife
1½ cups hot chicken stock or water
1½ tablespoons tomato paste
salt and freshly ground pepper
2 tablespoons flat-leaf parsley, finely chopped

Serves 6

1 Wash the chickens and pat dry with absorbent paper.
2 Rub salt and pepper all over them, including the cavity.
3 Place the chickens in a greased baking tin and pour over the oil.
4 Rub the oil all over the chickens with your hands, including the cavity.
5 Put a clove of crushed garlic into each cavity and tie the legs together with kitchen string.
6 Cover the chickens loosely with foil and bake in a preheated 90°C oven for 1 hour.
7 Remove the foil and increase the oven temperature to 200°C and cook for a further 45 minutes.
8 Remove from the oven and place onto another dish. Cover with the foil again, keep warm and set aside for 30 minutes.
9 To prepare the vegetables, cut the eggplant into bite-size chunks, sprinkle with salt and place into a colander for about 15 minutes.
10 Cut the zucchini into thick slices, sprinkle with salt and place into the colander with the eggplant.
11 Cut the red pepper in half, remove the seeds, then cut into thick strips. Cut the strips into bite-size pieces then set aside.
12 Heat the oil in a wok or saucepan then add the eggplant and onion, stirring to coat well with the oil. Cook on a medium heat for about 5 minutes, stirring frequently. Add the garlic, zucchini and red pepper and cook for a further 5 minutes.
13 Add the stock or water and tomato paste and cook for another 15 minutes on medium heat until sauce thickens and reduces slightly. Season with salt and pepper, add the parsley and stir through to mix well. Keep warm and set aside.

To serve: Put the chickens on a large warm serving dish and the vegetables in a bowl. Cut the chickens at the table and let everyone help themselves.

SPICY SPATCHCOCK WITH AVOCADO SALAD

2 spatchcocks

marinade

6 tablespoons light sour cream

2 tablespoons tomato kasoundi*

4 tablespoons coriander, chopped

salt and freshly ground pepper

salad

½ iceberg lettuce

2 large avocados

dressing

3 tablespoons olive oil

1 tablespoon coriander, chopped

1 small hot red chilli, seeds removed and finely chopped

juice ½ small lime

1 spring onion, finely sliced

salt and freshly ground pepper

Serves 4

1 Wash the spatchcocks and pat dry with absorbent paper.

2 Place each spatchcock on its breast and with kitchen scissors, cut along each side of the backbone and remove it. Turn each spatchcock over so that the breast is facing you and with the palm of your hand, gently press down to flatten, cracking the breastbone.

3 Insert your hand under the skin of each one, starting by loosening the skin near the neck and gradually pushing your hand through to separate the skin away from the breast and the thighs. Set aside.

4 Combine the sour cream, tomato kasoundi and coriander and season with salt and pepper. Stir to mix well.

5 Add the marinade mixture to the spatchcocks. Spread the marinade mixture with your hands in under the skin of the breast and all over the outside of the spatchcocks. Allow to marinate for 2 hours.

6 Preheat the chargrill then brush the grill with oil. Cook the spatchcocks on a low heat for about 20–30 minutes, brushing with a little oil while they are cooking. Take off the heat, set aside and keep warm for 15 minutes.

7 Wash and dry the lettuce and separate the leaves, leaving them whole. Place in a serving bowl.

8 Cut the avocados lengthwise into quarters and peel. Cut the quarters into thick slices and add to the lettuce.

9 Combine the oil, coriander, chilli, lime juice and spring onion and season with salt and pepper. Take the dressing to the table and add to the lettuce and avocado salad after you have served the spatchcocks as it can go soggy very quickly.

To serve: Cut the spatchcocks into 4 and place on a serving dish for everyone to help themselves. Add the dressing to the salad.

*Tomato kasoundi is available from good delis.

GRILLED QUAIL WITH HERBS AND CUCUMBER SALAD

6 quails

marinade

1 teaspoon whole coriander seeds

1 clove garlic, crushed

1 small hot red chilli, seeds removed and finely chopped

2 tablespoons flat-leaf parsley, finely chopped

1 tablespoon rosemary (leaves only)

6 tablespoons olive oil

salt and freshly ground pepper

4 sprigs rosemary

salad

1 telegraph cucumber, quartered lengthwise and cut into chunks

200 g yellow bell tomatoes

75 g black olives

1 small Spanish onion, halved and finely sliced

1 tablespoon fresh oregano (leaves only)

dressing

3 tablespoons olive oil

1 teaspoon lemon juice

salt and freshly ground pepper

Serves 6

1 Trim the neck flap from each quail.

2 Wash the quails under cold running water and pat dry with absorbent paper. Place in a large shallow dish.

3 Pound the coriander seeds in a mortar and combine with the rest of the marinade mixture (except for the 4 rosemary sprigs) and pour over the quails, turning them to coat well. Marinate overnight or for at least 3 hours. Bring quails back to room temperature before grilling.

4 Thread the quails onto 2 skewers (3 on each) with a rosemary sprig tucked between each one.

5 Preheat the chargrill then brush the grill with oil. Cook the quails on a medium to low heat breast-side down for about 5–6 minutes. Lightly brush the quails with oil and turn and cook for about another 4 minutes. Remove from the skewers and grill quickly on each side, brushing with oil before turning each time. Take off the heat and keep warm and set aside for 10 minutes.

6 Combine all of the salad ingredients in a serving bowl and pour over the dressing and season with salt and pepper. Toss to coat well.

To serve: Cut the quails in half and serve with the salad in the centre of 6 plates.

ROAST DUCK WITH CAVULISCEDDI AND CARAMELISED APPLE

2 x 2 kg ducks
3 tablespoons olive oil
2 cloves garlic
salt and freshly ground pepper
200 g onion, roughly chopped
100 g carrots, roughly chopped
100 g celery, roughly chopped

apples
500 g Granny Smith apples
2 tablespoons sugar
juice ½ lemon
2 tablespoons light olive oil

cavulisceddi*
300 g cavulisceddi (or baby bok choy)
2 tablespoons olive oil
1 teaspoon balsamic vinegar
1 clove garlic, finely sliced
salt and freshly ground pepper

sauce
1 cup dry white wine
1 cup apple juice
1 cup chicken stock

Serves 4

1 Cut off the necks and the wing tips from the ducks. Pull off the oil glands on either side of the tail openings and any other fatty bits and discard.
2 Wash the outside and cavity of each duck and thoroughly pat dry with absorbent paper.
3 Rub the outside and cavity with oil.
4 Put a garlic clove inside each cavity.
5 Season inside and out with salt and pepper.
6 Place the onion, carrots and celery in a roasting pan. Put a rack over the top and place each of the ducks (breast-side up) on the rack. Place in a pre-heated 220°C oven for 15 minutes.
7 Turn the oven down to 180°C and cook for about another 12 minutes or until breasts are medium rare.
8 Remove the ducks from the oven and cut the breasts off and set them aside.
9 Return the ducks to the oven (breast-side down) and cook for another 45 minutes until ducks are medium cooked.
10 Remove the ducks from the oven and cut off the leg portions. Set aside on another plate and keep warm.
11 Quarter the apples then peel and core them and cut into thick slices.
12 Place the apples into a bowl and sprinkle with sugar and lemon juice.
13 Heat the oil in a frying pan and cook the apples on a low heat (stirring to coat well) for about 5–7 minutes or until slightly mushy with a light caramelised colour. Set aside and keep warm.
14 Wash the cavulisceddi thoroughly. Heat the oil and balsamic vinegar in a wok or frying pan then add the garlic and cavulisceddi and stir to coat well.
15 Cover with a lid and cook for 2–3 minutes until the cavulisceddi starts to wilt. Season with salt and pepper and set aside.
16 To make the sauce, discard all the fat from the roasting pan. Place the pan over a medium to high heat on the stove. Add the wine and deglaze. Reduce by half and then add the apple juice. Reduce this by half and then add the chicken stock and reduce until it starts to thicken slightly. Strain through a fine sieve.

To serve: Put a leg portion in the centre of 4 plates. Carve the breasts diagonally into slices and place over the leg. Pour a little of the sauce around the meat. Serve the cavulisceddi and the apples in separate bowls for your guests to help themselves.

*Cavulisceddi leaves have a similar flavour to tender young, fresh radish leaves. Cavulisceddi can be purchased from good Italian greengrocers or better still, grow your own. My father grows them from seeds so they are ready to eat at the beginning of autumn. The seeds can be bought from an Italian deli. (If you can't get any cavulisceddi you can substitute baby bok choy.)

GRILLED DUCK WITH MASHED SWEET POTATO AND YELLOW BEANS

2 x 2 kg ducks

marinade

juice 8 oranges

4 tablespoons honey

2 cloves garlic, finely chopped

4 small hot red chillies, seeds removed and finely chopped

1 teaspoon garam masala

salt and freshly ground pepper

sweet potato

1 kg sweet potatoes

2 cloves garlic, unpeeled

salt and freshly ground pepper

4 tablespoons olive oil

2 tablespoons flat-leaf parsley, finely sliced

yellow beans

200 g yellow beans

2 tablespoons olive oil

¼ teaspoon lemon juice

1 clove garlic, finely sliced

salt and freshly ground black pepper

Serves 4

1 Cut off the necks and the wing tips from the ducks. Pull off the oil glands on either side of the tail openings and any other fatty bits and discard.
2 Wash the outside and cavity of each duck and thoroughly pat dry with absorbent paper.
3 Cut each duck into 4 and place in a large shallow dish.
4 Combine the orange juice, honey, garlic, chillies and garam masala. Season with salt and pepper and stir gently with a fork to mix well.
5 Pour the marinade over the ducks, mixing well to coat evenly. Set aside to marinate for at least 2 hours at room temperature or overnight in the fridge. Bring back to room temperature before cooking.
6 Preheat the chargrill. Brush the grill with oil and cook the ducks on a low heat. The pieces of duck will vary in their cooking times. The breast is delicious and tender cooked medium rare (just pink) and will take half the time of the legs and thighs which should be cooked to a little over medium. When cooked, take the breasts off the heat and brush lightly with oil. Cover with foil and a tea towel and set aside until the leg portions are done.
7 Peel and cut the sweet potatoes into large chunks and place in a saucepan with boiling water. Add the garlic and cook until the potatoes are soft and ready to mash.
8 Take off the heat. Remove the garlic and strain the potato chunks and return to the saucepan. Cut the end off each garlic clove and squeeze so that the garlic comes out over the potato. Season with salt and pepper.
9 Mash the lot with a potato masher and stir the oil through. Add the parsley and stir through. Cover to keep warm.
10 Heat the marinade mixture and simmer until it reduces slightly. Strain and set aside.
11 Meanwhile, steam the yellow beans. Heat the oil and lemon juice and fry the garlic for about 1 minute.
12 Place the beans in a serving bowl and pour over the oil, lemon juice and garlic and season with salt and pepper.

To serve: Cut the breasts diagonally into thin slices and place to one side of a serving dish. Place the leg portions to the side of the breast slices and pour a little of the marinade over the meat. Place the sweet potatoes in separate serving bowl and let everyone help themselves.

FISH AND SEAFOOD

I love the juices and scents of seafood grilled briefly over hot coals. When I was a kid, going to the beach was an adventure filled with anticipation and excitement. I would always wander amongst the rocks close to the shore with my bucket, collecting shells. As I turned, lifted and stirred my catch it was always the mussels I loved best. The packaging of mussels is simple, functional and elegant, protecting the most lovely of surprises. The first time I tasted mussels prepared on a barbecue grill was during the writing of this book. I was taken aback by the flavour as I tasted the first mussel straight off the grill. Like diving into the ocean, the mussel burst in my mouth with a rush.

Whenever the opportunity arises, my father and I go fishing for calamari off the Flinders Pier. With squid jiggers cleaned, prepared and hurled into the water my mind often drifts back to earlier trips when we would arrive home, sometimes in the middle of the night, to Mum waiting ready to cook the calamari. Mum and Dad would clean the calamari, cut them into pieces and place them in a shallow dish with flour. Mum would then quickly fry the calamari pieces in oil and season them with salt and plenty of freshly ground pepper. I still enjoy calamari cooked this way and often cook it for special occasions as the whole family loves it.

BREAKING UP TREVALLY

CHARGRILLED PRAWNS

SCALLOPS AND ARTICHOKES
READY TO BE CHARGRILLED

MARLIN STEAK CUT INTO
PIECES FOR THE ANTIPASTI OF
CHARGRILLED SEAFOOD
AND VEGETABLES

GRILLED TREVALLY WITH ROAST POTATOES

potatoes
600 g new potatoes washed, unpeeled, quartered
4 tablespoons olive oil
1 clove garlic, finely chopped
1 small hot red chilli, seeds removed, finely chopped
salt and freshly ground pepper
1 tablespoon flat-leaf parsley, chopped
2 tablespoons chives, cut into 2 cm segments

fish
4 trevally fillets, about 250 g each
2 oranges, sliced into 5 mm slices
2 lemons, sliced into 5 mm slices
2 limes, sliced into 5 mm slices

marinade
2 ripe tomatoes, chopped
1 clove garlic, finely chopped
1 tablespoon flat-leaf parsley, chopped
3 tablespoons olive oil
juice 1 lime
salt and freshly ground pepper

Serves 4

1 Place the potatoes on an oven tray. Pour over the oil, add the garlic and chilli and season with salt and pepper. Mix all of this thoroughly. Bake in a pre-heated 200°C oven for 1 hour.

2 Place the trevally fillets in a large shallow dish. Add the marinade ingredients, rub the mixture onto the fish with your hands and marinate for 45 minutes.

3 Preheat the chargrill. Top the grill with all the citrus slices and place the fillets skin-side down over the top. Cook the fish over a low heat for 5 minutes then gently turn over. After 2 minutes remove all the citrus slices and place them over the top of the fish like a covering and cook until fish is ready.

4 Take off the heat and place back into the dish with the marinade. Discard the citrus slices.

To serve: Place the fish in the centre of 4 warm plates and spoon a little of the marinade over the fish. Put the potatoes into a serving bowl and sprinkle with the parsley and chives.

GRILLED TREVALLY WITH SNOW PEAS AND TOMATOES

100 g snow peas
150 g inner leaves of cos lettuce

fish and marinade
1 trevally fillet (about 350 g)
1 tablespoon wild fennel leaves, finely chopped
1 tablespoon basil, finely sliced
juice ½ lemon
2 tablespoons olive oil
salt and freshly ground pepper

tomatoes
4 ripe roma tomatoes, quartered lengthwise
2 tablespoons olive oil
1 tablespoon wild fennel leaves, finely chopped
1 tablespoon basil, finely sliced
salt and freshly ground pepper
½ teaspoon sugar

Serves 4

1 Blanch the snow peas in boiling salted water for about 15 seconds. Refresh under cold running water then drain and set aside.

2 Wash the cos leaves, pat dry with absorbent paper and set aside.

3 Place the fish and all of the marinade ingredients in a shallow dish and mix well. Let this marinate for about 30 minutes.

4 In a flat shallow dish, combine the tomatoes the oil, fennel leaves, basil and salt and pepper. Turn the tomatoes to coat well. Place the tomatoes cut-side up and sprinkle evenly with the sugar.

5 Preheat the chargrill then brush the grill with oil. Grill the trevally fillet for about 2–3 minutes on each side or until it flakes away easily when pressed with a fork. Put the fish back in the dish with the marinade and set aside and allow to cool.

6 Grill the tomatoes on all sides (this won't take very long). Set aside in the same dish it came from.

7 Break the fish up with your fingers, making sure to remove any bones.

8 Place the fish in the dish with the tomatoes then add the snow peas and cos leaves and mix well.

To serve: Divide and place the fish and the snow pea and tomato salad in the centre of 4 plates. Serve with thick slices of crusty Italian-style bread.

KING GEORGE WHITING WITH SALSA VERDE AND ROAST POTATOES

potatoes

500 g potatoes, finely sliced

3 ripe tomatoes, finely sliced

1 small onion, finely sliced

4 tablespoons olive oil

salt and freshly ground pepper

salsa verde

6 anchovy fillets, finely chopped

2 cups flat-leaf parsley, finely chopped

1 tablespoon capers, rinsed

1 clove garlic, finely chopped

6 tablespoons olive oil

1 hard-boiled egg, finely chopped

1 teaspoon lemon juice

salt and freshly ground pepper

whiting

4 King George whiting (about 350 g each), scaled and cleaned

4 tablespoons olive oil

juice 1 lemon

salt and freshly ground pepper

Serves 4

1 Place the potatoes, tomatoes and onion slices in a baking tray and pour over the oil. Season with salt and pepper and mix all the ingredients with your hands. Bake in a preheated 180°C oven for 1¼ hours.

2 To prepare the salsa verde, put the anchovies, parsley, capers and garlic into a bowl and stir thoroughly.

3 Start adding the oil a little at a time, stirring constantly and vigorously until all the oil is used.

4 Stir in the egg and lemon juice then season with salt and pepper and set aside.

5 Wash the whiting and pat dry with absorbent paper. Cut 3 shallow diagonal slashes across the thickest part of each fish. Place them in a shallow dish then add the oil and lemon juice, season with salt and pepper and rub all over to coat well.

6 When the potatoes are nearly ready, place the fish on a preheated, oiled chargrill. On a medium to low heat, cook the fish for about 3–4 minutes on each side. Be careful to turn the fish gently when the first side is cooked. Brush this side with some of the oil and lemon left in the dish.

7 When other side is cooked, brush this side with the oil and lemon and set aside and keep warm.

To serve: Place the King George whiting in the centre of 4 warmed plates. Spread a little of the salsa verde across the top half of each fish and serve the rest of the salsa in a small bowl at the table. Serve the potatoes in a bowl.

OCEAN TROUT WITH BOK CHOY

4 ocean trout fillets (200 g each), skin on

marinade

4 medium-size lemon leaves, crushed
juice 2 large oranges
salt and freshly ground black pepper
25 g butter
½ cup dry white wine

bok choy

2 tablespoons olive oil
1 teaspoon ginger, finely chopped
1 bunch baby bok choy, trimmed, cut lengthwise
salt and freshly ground pepper

Serves 4

1 Place the trout fillets in a large shallow dish.
2 Add the lemon leaves on and around the fish.
3 Pour over the orange juice and season with salt and pepper. Set aside and let this marinate for 1 hour. (Leave the butter and wine for later.)
4 Heat the oil in a wok then add the ginger and cook for about 1 minute.
5 Add the bok choy and cook on a low heat for about 10–15 minutes. Season with salt and pepper then set aside and keep warm.
6 Preheat the chargrill then turn the heat down low and brush the grill with oil. Cook the trout skin-side down for about 3–4 minutes, then gently turn and cook the other side for about 2 minutes. Take off the heat and keep warm.
7 Melt the butter in a frying pan and add what is left of the marinade mixture. Cook this for about 1 minute then add the wine.
8 Simmer and let the liquid reduce by half and strain through a fine sieve. Set aside and keep warm.

To serve: Divide the bok choy in the middle of 4 warm plates. Place a trout fillet on top and leaning to one side of the bok choy then pour over the reduced marinade liquid and serve.

GRILLED TUNA WITH EGGS AND CAPERS

4 eggs
2 lemons
1 bunch chives
1 tablespoon capers
4 yellow fin tuna steaks, about 200 g each

marinade
4 tablespoons olive oil
juice ½ lemon
salt and freshly ground pepper

mayonnaise
2 egg yolks
¼ teaspoon salt
¾ cup olive oil
juice ½ lemon

Serves 4

1 Boil the eggs until just hard boiled. Set aside to cool then shell and quarter lengthwise.
2 Quarter the lemons lengthwise and set aside.
3 Finely chop the chives and set aside. (Reserve 12 stems of the chives for garnish.)
4 Rinse the capers under cold running water then pat dry with absorbent paper and set aside.
5 Place the tuna in a shallow dish and pour over the oil and lemon juice. Season with salt and pepper and marinate for half an hour.
6 Meanwhile, to prepare the mayonnaise, make sure that all items are at room temperature. Place the egg yolks and salt in a bowl and stir thoroughly with a wooden spoon or wire whisk until the mixture has a smooth consistency and has become slightly paler. (Place a folded tea towel under the bowl to stop it from moving around too much.)
7 Add the oil a drop at a time ensuring that it is being absorbed completely. Once the mixture starts to thicken, the oil can be added in a slow, thin drizzle.
8 When a third of the oil has been combined, add the lemon juice a little at a time. Continue adding the rest of the oil until it is all absorbed.
9 Preheat the chargrill. Brush the grill with oil and cook the tuna for about 1 minute on each side—it should be quite rare. Take tuna off the heat and place back into the marinade mixture.
10 Grill the lemon wedges and set aside.

To serve: Combine the hard-boiled eggs with the mayonnaise and chopped chives and stir gently to mix well. Divide the mixture onto the centre of 4 plates. Put some capers on top of the eggs and cut each tuna steak in half and place over the eggs. Top the tuna with the lemon wedges and garnish with the remaining chives.

GRILLED SARDINES WITH WALNUTS AND ITALIAN OAK LETTUCE AND OLIVE SALAD

16 fresh sardine fillets
salt and freshly ground pepper

walnut stuffing
3 tablespoons olive oil
1 clove garlic, finely chopped
50 g walnuts, finely chopped
1 cup white breadcrumbs
2 tablespoons flat-leaf parsley, finely chopped
salt and freshly ground pepper

salad
1 Italian oak lettuce
12 black pitted olives
2 tablespoons olive oil
juice ½ lemon
salt and freshly ground pepper

Serves 4

1 Wash the sardine fillets and pat dry on absorbent paper.
2 To prepare the walnut stuffing, heat the oil in a frying pan then add the garlic and cook on a low heat for 30 seconds or until the garlic turns white.
3 Add the walnuts, breadcrumbs and parsley and cook for about 5 minutes or until the breadcrumbs are golden brown. Season with salt and pepper and set aside.
4 Preheat the chargrill then brush the grill with oil.
5 Season the sardine fillets with salt and pepper. Place half the fillets skin-side down on the grill. It is best to cook the sardines in 2 lots as they cook very quickly. By the time you have placed the last fillet the first one should be ready to turn. The fillets should cook for about 1 minute on each side. Place the fillets back onto the tray skin-side down and continue to grill the other half. Set aside and keep warm.
6 Wash the lettuce leaves and dry on absorbent paper.
7 Place the lettuce in a bowl with the olives. Dress with the oil and lemon juice and season with salt and pepper.

To serve: Spoon a little pile of the salad onto the centre of 4 plates. On either side of this place a sardine fillet skin-side down. Divide and spoon the walnut mixture on top and cover with the other sardine fillets.

GRILLED CALAMARI WITH LEMON, OLIVE OIL AND BALSAMIC VINEGAR

4 calamari tubes (about 150 g each)
2 tablespoons olive oil
1 tablespoon balsamic vinegar
cracked pepper

marinade
juice 1 lemon
4 tablespoons olive oil
salt and freshly ground pepper

Serves 4

1 Cut each calamari tube lengthwise so it is in 1 large piece. Cut each piece in half and trim the ends.
2 Score the inside of each calamari piece in a crisscross pattern with a sharp knife and place in a large shallow dish. Pour over the marinade mixture and mix well. Leave to marinate for 15 minutes.
3 Preheat the chargrill then brush the grill with oil. Grill the calamari score-side down for about 2 minutes. Turn and grill the other side. It will curl up almost straightaway. As soon as it does, take it off the heat.

To serve: Place 2 pieces of calamari in the centre of 4 plates. Pour over the oil and vinegar and sprinkle with cracked pepper. Serve with lemon wedges, a tossed salad and thick slices of crusty Italian-style bread.

CORIANDER BABY OCTOPUS WITH GRILLED MUSSELS

1 kg baby octopus

½ kg fresh mussels

marinade

6 tablespoons olive oil

zest of 1 lemon, minced

2 small hot red chillies, seeds removed and finely chopped

2 cloves garlic, finely chopped

1 tablespoon ginger, finely chopped

3 tablespoons coriander, chopped

salt and freshly ground pepper

1 cup dry white wine

½ kg ripe tomatoes skinned, seeded, coarsely chopped

Serves 6

1 Wash the octopus, pat dry with absorbent paper then place in a large bowl and set aside.

2 Scrub the mussel shells with a stiff brush under cold running water and pull hard to remove the beards. (Discard any mussels that are open.) Set aside.

3 Add all the marinade ingredients (except the wine, tomatoes, salt and pepper) to the bowl with the baby octopus. Mix well to coat all over and marinate for 30 minutes. Remove the octopus and set the marinade mixture aside for later.

4 Place the baby octopus on a preheated chargrill. Cook for about 6–8 minutes on each side, depending on the size. Set aside in a warm bowl.

5 Grill the mussels on a high heat on the barbecue. As they open take them off the heat and add to the bowl with the octopus.

6 Heat the marinade mixture in a frying pan then add the wine and the juices from the bowl with the octopus and mussels. Simmer until the liquid has reduced by half.

7 Add the tomatoes and cook for about 2 minutes. Season with salt and pepper.

8 Pour the marinade over the octopus and mussels and stir through.

To serve: Leave everything in the bowl and let everyone help themselves. Serve with a loaf of thick crusty Italian-style bread. Supply finger bowls and small hand towels.

GRILLED SCALLOPS WITH ARTICHOKES

4 artichokes
juice ½ lemon
24 fresh scallops
marinade
4 tablespoons olive oil
¼ teaspoon balsamic vinegar
1 tablespoon shallots, finely chopped
4 ripe tomatoes, skin and seeds removed, coarsely chopped
salt and freshly ground pepper
6 basil leaves

Serves 4

1 Cut the stems off the artichokes and remove the outer leaves until you have the tender inner leaves only.
2 Cut 2.5 cm from the tops to remove the darker and spiky tipped portion of the leaves.
3 Slice each artichoke into 6.
4 Place the artichoke pieces and lemon juice in a saucepan of boiling water. Turn the heat down and simmer for 5 minutes.
5 Remove the artichoke pieces from the saucepan and refresh under cold water. Set aside.
6 Remove the scallops from their shells. To clean the scallops, remove the brown slushy bit between the orange coral and the white muscle. Then with kitchen scissors, cut the hard white portion attached to the edge of each scallop.
7 Combine all the marinade ingredients in a bowl. Add the scallops. Stir gently to coat everything well and marinate for 30 minutes.
8 Remove the scallops only and reserve the marinade for later.
9 Preheat the chargrill. Brush the grill with oil and on a medium to high heat grill the scallops for 1 minute. Take off the heat and keep warm.
10 Brush the artichokes with oil and grill for 2–3 minutes on each side then set aside.

To serve: Pour the marinade mixture onto the centre of 4 plates. Alternate 6 artichoke pieces and 6 scallops in a circle on each plate.

GRILLED PRAWNS WITH MINT AND GINGER

28 green king prawns

marinade

3 tablespoons fresh mint leaves, roughly torn

2 tablespoons fresh ginger, finely chopped

2 small hot red chillies, seeds removed and finely chopped

1 clove garlic, finely chopped

juice 1 lime

3 tablespoons olive oil

salt and freshly ground pepper

bread

4 thick slices of crusty Italian-style bread

2 tablespoons olive oil

freshly ground pepper

sauce

50 g butter

1 cup dry white wine

Serves 4

1 Remove the heads from the prawns and peel the shells down to the last small section before the tail.

2 Once the heads have been removed the intestinal tracts will be exposed. Grab this with your thumb and forefinger and gently pull to devein the prawn. (It will come out quite easily.) Trim the head end then place all the prawns in a large shallow dish. Set the heads and shells aside.

3 Add the mint, ginger, chillies, garlic, lime juice and oil to the prawns. Season with salt and pepper. Coat the prawns well with the marinade mixture and marinate for 1 hour.

4 Preheat the chargrill then brush the grill with oil. Brush the bread with oil and season with lots of pepper. Grill the bread then cut lengthwise on the diagonal and set aside.

5 Grill the prawns for about 2-3 minutes on each side then set aside and keep warm.

6 To make the sauce, melt the butter in a frying pan and add what is left of the marinade mixture, plus the prawn heads and shells. Cook this for about 1 minute then add the wine. Simmer and let the liquid reduce by half then strain it through a fine sieve.

To serve: Divide and stack the prawns in the middle of 4 warm plates and place the bread pieces on top of each other to one side. Pour the sauce over the prawns and serve.

GINGER AND CORIANDER PRAWNS WITH ROCKET AND CUCUMBER SALAD

12 green king prawns

marinade

2 small hot red chillies, seeds removed and finely chopped
1 small brown onion, finely chopped
1 tablespoon fresh ginger, finely chopped
3 tablespoons fresh coriander, finely chopped
1 clove garlic, finely chopped
1 teaspoon cumin powder
4 tablespoons grapeseed oil
salt and freshly ground pepper

sauce

2 tablespoons grapeseed oil
2 ripe tomatoes, skin and seeds removed, coarsely chopped
1 cup coconut milk
salt and freshly ground pepper

salad

50 g rocket
1 Lebanese cucumber, quartered lengthwise, cut into 1 cm slices

dressing

2 tablespoons olive oil
juice ½ lemon
salt and freshly ground pepper

Serves 4

1 Combine the prawns and all the marinade ingredients in a large shallow dish. Leave to marinate for 1 hour.
2 Remove the prawns from the marinade and set aside.
3 To prepare the sauce, heat the oil in a frying pan and add all of the marinade ingredients. Gently cook this for about 2–3 minutes, stirring continuously.
4 Add the tomatoes and cook for a further 5 minutes.
5 Add the coconut milk and cook gently, stirring occasionally, to reduce by half.
6 Strain the sauce through a fine sieve into a bowl ready for serving. Set aside and keep warm.
7 Preheat the chargrill then brush the grill with oil. Grill the prawns for about 2–3 minutes on each side then set aside and keep warm.
8 To prepare the salad, combine the rocket, cucumber and dressing in a bowl. Mix well.

To serve: Pile the rocket and cucumber salad in the centre of 4 plates then place 3 prawns on top of each. Serve the coconut sauce separately. Supply finger bowls and warm towels.

ANTIPASTI OF CHARGRILLED SEAFOOD AND VEGETABLES

6 mussels
4 tablespoons olive oil
juice ½ lemon
salt and freshly ground pepper
6 green king prawns
1 small hot red chilli, seeds removed and finely chopped
200 g marlin steak
1 clove garlic
¼ cup basil leaves, torn
6 asparagus spears
200 g eggplant
6 oysters
6 slices smoked salmon
wedges of lemon

Serves 6

1 Scrub the mussel shells with a stiff brush under cold running water and pull hard to remove the beards. (Discard any mussels that are open).
2 Preheat the chargrill. Brush the grill with oil and grill the mussels on a high heat. As they open, take them off the heat and place in a bowl. Add 2 tablespoons of the oil, 1 tablespoon of the lemon juice, season with salt and pepper and stir through the mussels. Set aside.
3 Remove the heads from the prawns and peel the shells down to the last small section before the tail.
4 Once the head has been removed the intestinal tract will be exposed. Grab this with your thumb and forefinger and gently pull to devein the prawn. (It will come out quite easily.) Trim the head end then place the prawns in a shallow dish and add the chopped chilli and 1 tablespoon of oil. Season with salt and pepper.
5 Grill the prawns for about 2–3 minutes on each side then place back in the bowl with the oil and chilli and set aside.
6 Cut the marlin steak into bite-size pieces and marinate with the garlic, basil and 1 tablespoon of oil. Season with salt and pepper.
7 Grill the marlin pieces for about 1–2 minutes on each side then place back in the bowl with the marinade mixture and set aside.
8 Wash the asparagus and trim the ends. Place in boiling salted water and cook for about 2–3 minutes. Drain and place straight onto the chargrill, brushing with oil as they are cooking. Set aside.
9 Cut the eggplant into 1 cm discs then salt both sides and place on absorbent paper. Leave for 15 minutes.
10 Brush the preheated grill with oil.
11 Brush the eggplant slices with oil and grill until they are cooked. Set aside.

To serve: Place the oysters in the centre of a large white dish. Arrange the smoked salmon to one side of them. Continue to arrange the rest of the seafood and grilled vegetables around the edge of the dish. Serve with wedges of lemon.

DESSERTS

By the time dessert comes around everyone has uncoiled and relaxed. Soft cheeses, ripe fresh fruit and spoonfuls of creamy, soft cakes leave everyone feeling at peace with the world.

One of my earliest memories is of watching my father at the back of his fruit shop quickly cutting through the middle of small rockmelons with his large steel knife. He would then spoon out the seeds and heap spoonfuls of vanilla icecream inside each juicy melon half. There we would sit, Mum, Dad, my brother and I, mouths full and with sweet juices running down the sides of our mouths and under our chins. When our family gets together now there are so many of us that a variety of succulent melons is always cut and served as a healthy dessert.

The recipe for that classic Sicilian pastry, cannoli, Ricotta Cream Filled Cones (page 118), is a traditional family one of my mother's. However, while the ingredients here are the same as Mum's, the shape is inspired by Christine Manfield. The heights Chris achieves with her desserts has inspired me to try something a little different with my mother's cannoli, shaping them into cones and serving them standing up dusted with icing sugar.

Cheese and fruit at the end of a meal is a wonderful way to extend a lunch with friends into dinner. One of my favourite places is the The Richmond Hill Cafe and Larder in Melbourne. As you enter the cafe the black waiting staff are like a blur of bees gently moving about their business. The aromas which come from their cheese room take your breath away. The selection of good things to help you wind down on page 130 is inspired by the cafe. Coulommiers is a soft, white mould cheese made from cow's milk, and a very old member of the brie family. It is made in Ile-de-France, 1 hour's drive outside Paris, by the Rouzaire family. Maggie Beer's quince paste shaped into quenelles is the perfect partner for this lovely ripe, soft cheese.

CUTTING BISCOTTI

FOR LEMON AND LIME TEA GRANITA

FRESH BERRY TRIFLE

ORANGE AND GREEN MELON BALLS IN
WATERMELON JELLY WITH ZABAGLIONE

A CORELLA PEAR

GRILLED NECTARINES WITH BAKED RICOTTA

ricotta
450 g ricotta
2 tablespoons castor sugar
1 egg
¼ teaspoon grated lemon rind
1 teaspoon dry marsala

nectarines
2 tablespoons dry marsala
1 tablespoon castor sugar
3 ripe nectarines, about 150 g each

Serves 6

1 Combine the ricotta, sugar, egg, grated lemon rind and marsala in a bowl. Stir well with a fork or wire whisk until smooth and creamy then set aside. (For a creamier ricotta mixture, rest the ricotta overnight over a fine sieve lined with muslin.)

2 Fill 6 lightly greased mould tins (7 cm diameter, 5 cm deep) with the ricotta cream and place in a bain-marie (a baking dish with enough hot water to reach halfway up the metal moulds).

3 Bake in a preheated 180°C oven for 40–45 minutes.

4 Remove the ricotta creams in their moulds from the bain-marie and let cool.

5 Meanwhile, heat the marsala and sugar for the nectarines in a saucepan until all the sugar dissolves and the mixture reduces slightly. Set aside.

6 Cut the cheeks from the nectarines.

7 Preheat the chargrill then brush the grill with grapeseed oil.

8 Brush the cut sides of the nectarines with the syrup and grill until you have the golden marks from the grill bars.

To serve: Remove the ricotta cream from the moulds and place in the centre of 6 individual bowls. Place a nectarine half alongside.

RICOTTA CREAM FILLED CONES

cones
3 tablespoons white wine
1 tablespoon sugar
250 g plain flour, sifted
2 egg yolks, reserving the egg whites
1 tablespoon olive oil
2 cups of olive oil for frying
icing sugar

ricotta cream
300 g ricotta
1 tablespoon sugar
½ teaspoon grated lemon rind
1 tablespoon dark chocolate, grated

Serves 8

1 To make the cones, heat the wine and sugar in a saucepan until the sugar dissolves and the liquid comes to the boil. Set aside to cool.
2 To make the dough, place the flour on a floured surface and make a well in the centre. Add the egg yolks and oil and with your fingers gradually incorporate them with a little of the flour. Add the wine and sugar mixture and mix well. Knead the dough for 5 minutes.
3 Roll out the dough with a rolling pin and cut into 4 portions. Flatten each portion with a rolling pin to a 5 mm-thick rectangular shape.
4 Roll through a hand pasta machine 10 times at the highest setting, folding the dough over as you go.
5 Roll each portion through a second time, 1½ notches from the lowest setting. Do this 10 times, folding the dough over as you go. Place each of the dough sheets between clean, dry tea towels.

6 Lightly grease 4 metal cream horn moulds. (You will have to prepare and fry the cones in batches of 4.)

7 To make the cones, cut a straight edge at the end of the dough sheet and align the horn mould with this edge (with the wide open end facing you).

8 Lift and wrap the straight edge of the dough around the metal mould allowing a little of the dough to overlap for the join.

9 Dip your finger in some egg white and brush along both the edges that are to join and then press down lightly to seal. Continue preparing the rest of the moulds. (Keep any scraps of dough to incorporate again through the pasta machine.)

10 Heat the oil in a saucepan to just boiling point and then turn down to low. Make sure there is enough oil to cover the shells.

11 Fry the shells, turning them over as each half cooks to a golden brown. Place on absorbent paper to cool and set aside. Repeat until all the dough has been used. (This should make 16 cones.)

12 Combine the ricotta, sugar, lemon rind and chocolate in a bowl. Stir thoroughly with a fork or spoon until quite smooth and creamy. The sugar will dissolve within minutes. Cover with cling wrap and place in the fridge. (For a creamier ricotta mixture, rest the ricotta overnight over a fine sieve lined with muslin.)

13 Just before serving, fill each of the cones with the ricotta cream. Dust with icing sugar and place on a serving dish.

To serve: Place in the centre of the table so everyone can help themselves or serve 2 on individual plates. Serve with good, strong black coffee.

INDIVIDUAL ORANGE CAKES WITH MASCARPONE

cake
250 g self-raising flour
pinch salt
200 g soft butter
150 g castor sugar
5 eggs
½ cup fresh orange juice, strained
grated rind 1 orange

mascarpone cream
450 g mascarpone cream
100 ml thickened cream
1 tablespoon castor sugar
2 tablespoons Grand Marnier

orange syrup
½ cup fresh orange juice, strained
120 g sugar
1 tablespoon Grand Marnier

Serves 8

1 Preheat the oven to 170°C. Grease 8 small 10 x 5.5 cm loaf tins.
2 Sift flour and salt together.
3 Cream the butter and sugar in an electric mixer for about 5 minutes or until pale and fluffy.
4 Beat the eggs in 1 at a time so that each egg is mixed in well.
5 Add the orange juice, grated orange rind and flour alternately, mixing gently after each addition using a wooden spoon or spatula until well incorporated.
6 Spoon the batter into the individual loaf tins and bake in the oven for 20 minutes or until golden on top. Remove cakes from the oven and leave in their tins to cool a little (about 5 minutes). Remove from tins and rest on a wire rack to cool.
7 To make the mascarpone cream, in an electric mixer, combine the mascarpone, cream, sugar and Grand Marnier and beat until thick.
8 For the orange syrup, heat all the ingredients until sugar dissolves.
9 Brush each of the cakes with the orange syrup and then cover all over with the mascarpone cream.

To serve: Place an individual cake in the centre of 8 plates and sprinkle with icing sugar.

LEMON AND LIME TEA GRANITA WITH BISCOTTI

4 cups weak black tea
¾ cup sugar
½ cup fresh lemon juice, strained
½ cup fresh lime juice, strained
¼ teaspoon of grated lemon and lime zest
biscotti
2 eggs
1½ tablespoons grapeseed oil
1½ tablespoons milk
1 tablespoon castor sugar
200 g self-raising flour
¼ teaspoon of grated lemon and lime zest
icing
100 g sugar
1½ tablespoons water

Serves 8

1 In a saucepan, heat the tea and sugar together and cook until it just comes to the boil and the sugar has dissolved. Let this cool.
2 Add the lemon and lime juice and the zest and stir well.
3 Pour mixture into a shallow metal dish or cake tin and place in the freezer.
4 Stir every half an hour with a fork to break up the ice crystals. These will have formed around the edge of the dish, so scrape and break up the ice all around the sides, stirring this in towards the middle of the dish. The granita is ready once all the liquid has solidified—this usually takes about 2–3 hours. If you are not ready to serve the granita, keep stirring it every half an hour or alternatively, make it the day before and store in an airtight plastic or glass container.
5 To make the biscotti, first preheat the oven to 180°C.
6 In a bowl, combine the eggs, oil, milk and sugar and beat until well mixed and frothy.
7 Fold in the flour and the lemon and lime zest and mix until well combined.
8 On a floured surface, knead the dough for 5 minutes. Then roll the dough into a sausage shape, about 40 cm long.
9 Press down and flatten the dough until it is 1 cm thick. Cut in half, and then cut each portion into 12 slices (for 24 biscuits).
10 Place the biscuits on a greased baking tray and cook for about 10–12 minutes or until light golden brown. Allow to cool.
11 To make the icing, heat the sugar and water together in a saucepan until it reaches boiling point. Pour over the biscuits. With a spatula or with your hands, gently turn the biscuits over and over until the syrup starts to cool and turn white. Be patient as this takes about 8–10 minutes. Store in an airtight container.

To serve: Break up and stir the granita and spoon it into 8 bowls, glasses or cups and serve with the biscotti.

FRESH BERRY TRIFLE

3 tablespoons dry marsala
1 cup espresso coffee
12–15 savoiardi biscuits (sponge fingers)
mascarpone cream
3 egg yolks
2 tablespoons castor sugar
500 g mascarpone
300 ml thickened cream
berries
1 punnet raspberries
1 punnet blackberries
2 punnets strawberries

Serves 6

1 Combine the marsala and coffee.
2 Dip the biscuits into the marsala and coffee and arrange half the biscuits in the bottom of a glass serving bowl with a 19 cm diameter. (You may have to cut the biscuits on the outer edge so that they lie flat in the bowl.)
3 Beat the egg yolks and sugar in a mixing bowl until they are light and creamy.
4 Add the mascarpone and cream and beat until smooth and creamy.
5 Spread the raspberries over the top of the biscuits.
6 Pour half the mascarpone cream mixture over the raspberries.
7 Spread the blackberries over the top of the mascarpone cream.
8 Place the remaining biscuits which have been dipped into the marsala and coffee in another layer.
9 Spread the rest of the mascarpone cream over the biscuits.
10 For the top layer, arrange all the strawberries to cover the cream.
11 Cover with cling wrap and place in the fridge until ready to serve. (This recipe should be made at least 6 hours before it is to be served, or the night before, to allow the trifle to set and all the flavours to blend together.)

To serve: Scoop out the trifle onto 6 plates with a large serving spoon.

PANETTONE WITH BLACKBERRIES, RASPBERRIES AND STRAWBERRIES

500 g panettone*
3 tablespoons madeira or dry sherry
4 tablespoons castor sugar
1 teaspoon cinnamon
berries
150 g blackberries
150 g raspberries
400 g small strawberries
2 tablespoons icing sugar

Serves 8

1 Cut the panettone into 8 wedges.
2 Brush the cut sides with the madeira and sprinkle with 2 tablespoons of the castor sugar. Set aside.
3 Place the blackberries, raspberries and strawberries in a large shallow dish and sprinkle with the icing sugar. Set aside.
4 Preheat the chargrill then brush the grill with grapeseed oil. Grill the panettone wedges over a medium heat until they are toasted and the sugar has caramelised. Take off the heat and set aside.
5 Mix the cinnamon and the rest of the castor sugar and place onto a flat plate. Spread out to cover the plate and dip both sides of the panettone wedges. Set aside.

To serve: Place a panettone portion to one side of each plate. Divide and drop the berries over the top. Serve with thickened cream.

*Panettone, more a sweet bread than a cake, is traditionally given as a gift at Christmas in the shape of a tall domed tower or at Easter shaped like a dove. It has a light texture, studded with raisins and candied fruit, and can be bought from Italian delis or good food stores.

ORANGE AND GREEN MELON BALLS IN WATERMELON JELLY WITH ZABAGLIONE

1½ kg watermelon
8 gelatine leaves
800 g rockmelon
800 g honeydew melon

zabaglione
4 egg yolks
3 tablespoons castor sugar
1 tablespoon dry marsala

Serves 6

1 Cut the watermelon into thick slices and remove the rind and as many seeds as you can. Cut into chunks and place the flesh into a blender and puree.
2 Strain the watermelon puree through a fine sieve covered with 3 layers of muslin placed over a bowl. (Do not try to press the puree, just leave it.) Discard the solids and strain the the juice twice more through the layers of muslin.
3 This should yield about 3 cups of liquid. Set aside.
4 To make the jelly, soak the gelatine leaves in a shallow dish of cold water for about 5–6 minutes. Meanwhile, heat 1 cup of watermelon juice in a saucepan. Squeeze the gelatine leaves, place in the heated juice and stir briskly with a fork. (The leaves should dissolve straightaway.) Pour the mixture into the rest of the watermelon juice, stirring all the time. Set aside in the fridge while you prepare the melon balls.
5 Remove the seeds from the rockmelon and honeydew melon.
6 Make 12 melon balls from each of the melons with a melon baller.
7 Pour equal quantities of the watermelon jelly into 6 glasses, filling just under two thirds of each glass.
8 Add 2 of each of the melon balls into the 6 glasses. Cover with cling wrap and chill to set the jelly. (This should take about 2–3 hours.)
9 To make the zabaglione, beat the egg yolks and sugar in the top part of a double saucepan with an electric hand mixer or wire wisk until they are pale and creamy.
10 Place over just simmering water in the bottom part of the saucepan and beat constantly, gradually adding the marsala until the zabaglione begins to thicken to a light, soft texture and increase in volume (this should take about 8–10 minutes).
11 Take off the heat and place the top part of the saucepan into a large bowl of cold water, beating continually with a wooden spoon while the zabaglione cools down a little.

To serve: Pour the warm zabaglione over the orange and green melon balls in watermelon jelly and serve immediately.

COULOMMIERS WITH CORELLA PEARS AND MAGGIE BEER'S QUINCE PASTE

12 thin slices crusty white bread
3 corella pears
500 g coulommiers (or your favourite ripe soft cheese at room temperature)
100 g Maggie Beer's quince paste (from selected delis)

Serves 6

1 Preheat the chargrill then brush the grill with oil. Grill the bread until it is golden. Set aside to cool.
2 Choose a large platter or wicker tray. (You may wish to line the tray with vine or fig leaves.)
3 Shape the quince paste into quenelles by filling a large spoon with the paste, then dipping another spoon into boiling water and inverting it over the spoon with quince paste to mould the paste into an oval shape. Slide straight onto a plate and set aside.

To serve: Arrange the bread, pears, cheese, and quince-paste quenelles on the tray and supply individual plates, knives and forks.

APPLE AND FIG CAKE WITH CHESTNUTS

1 kg Granny Smith apples
2 tablespoons sugar
1 teaspoon cinnamon
1 tablespoon light olive oil
300 g fresh figs

cake batter
80 g soft butter
70 g castor sugar
1 egg, lightly beaten
200 g self-raising flour, sifted
½ cup milk
2 tablespoons apple juice

chestnuts
150 g chestnuts
1 tablespoon salt

Serves 8

1 Cut the apples into quarters and remove the cores. Peel and cut into thick even slices.
2 Place into a bowl and sprinkle with sugar and cinnamon.
3 Heat the oil in a frying pan then add the apples and cook on a low heat, stirring to coat with the oil. Cook for about 5 minutes then set aside to cool.
4 Peel the figs and cut in half lengthwise. Set aside.
5 Grease a ceramic or glass baking dish with butter and place the apples in an even layer. Spread the figs over the top then set aside.
6 Cream the butter and sugar on a low speed in a mixing bowl until pale and fluffy.
7 Add the egg gradually and mix so that it is well incorporated.
8 Add the flour, milk and apple juice alternately, stirring with a wooden spoon until mixture is well blended.
9 Spoon the batter evenly over the top of the apples and figs and bake in a preheated 180°C oven for 30 minutes or until golden on top.
10 Remove the cake from the oven and leave in its dish to cool a little.
11 Make a cut in each of the chestnuts and place them into a baking dish. Sprinkle with salt and place in a preheated 200°C oven for 20 minutes. Remove from the oven and cool.
12 Peel the chestnuts and chop finely.
13 Preheat a saucepan and dry-roast the chestnuts over a high heat until they are a light golden colour. Set aside to cool.

To serve: Spoon the cake into separate bowls or plates and serve with thick cream and sprinkled with chestnuts.

INDEX

Antipasti of chargrilled seafood and
vegetables 110
Apple and fig cake with chestnuts 132
Apples with Italian sausages and
hazelnuts 52
Artichoke
frittata, Pina's 32
with grilled scallops 105
Asparagus and long green peppers 28

Basil mayonnaise, with chicken breast
and cos salad 66
Berry
trifle, fresh 125
Panettone with blackberries,
raspberries and strawberries 126
Bok choy with ocean trout 95
Broad beans with lamb cutlets and
potato patties 42

Calamari grilled, with lemon, olive oil
and balsamic vinegar 100
Cavulisceddi
and goat's cheese frittata 34
with roast duck and caramelised
apple 81
Chicken
breast with basil mayonnaise and
cos salad 66
breast with ricotta and spinach 64
burgers with grilled vegetables 73
drumsticks, macadamia-stuffed 68
liver, orange, rocket and
pomegranate salad 12
thighs stuffed with lime and baby
beets 71
Coriander baby octopus with grilled
mussels 102
Coulommiers with corella pears and
Maggie Beer's quince paste 130
Cucumber salad, with grilled quail and
herbs 78

Diego's mixed green salad 5
Duck
grilled, with mashed sweet potato
and yellow beans 82
roast, with cavulisceddi and
caramelised apple 81

Eggplant and green bean salad 11
Eggplant
Palmina's charcoal, and tomato 20
with penne, spinach and tomato 23
with rack of lamb and rosemary
walnut pesto 41
with roast chicken, zucchini and red
peppers 74
Eggs, with grilled tuna and capers 96
Eye fillet with tomato, oregano and
boiled potatoes 47

Fig and apple cake with chestnuts 132
Fresh berry trifle 125
Frittata
artichoke, Pina's 32
Cavulisceddi and goat's cheese
frittata 34

Garlic and rosemary roast potatoes,
with Italian sausages 55
Ginger
and coriander prawns with rocket
and cucumber salad 108
and mint with grilled prawns 107
Goat's cheese
and grilled zucchini on barbecued
bread 27
frittata and cavulisceddi 34
Green bean salad, and eggplant 11
Grilled calamari with lemon, olive oil
and balsamic vinegar 100
Grilled duck with mashed sweet
potato and yellow beans 82
Grilled nectarines with baked ricotta 116

Grilled prawns with mint and ginger 107
Grilled quail with herbs and cucumber
salad 78
Grilled sardines with walnuts and
Italian oak lettuce and olive salad 99
Grilled scallops with artichokes 105
Grilled trevally with roast potatoes 89
Grilled trevally with snow peas and
tomatoes 90
Grilled tuna with eggs and capers 96
Grilled vegetables on rocket and ricotta 24
Grilled zucchini and goat's cheese on
barbecued bread 27

Individual orange cakes with
mascarpone 121
Italian sausages with apples and
hazelnuts 52
Italian sausages with garlic and
rosemary roast potatoes 55

King George whiting with salsa verde
and roast potatoes 92

Lamb
cutlets with broad beans and potato
patties 42
rack of, with eggplants and
rosemary walnut pesto 41
rosemary and garlic stuffed, with
spinach and red pepper sauce 44
Lemon and lime tea granita with
biscotti 122
Lentil salad 8
Lime
and lemon tea granita with biscotti 122
chicken thighs stuffed with, and
baby beets 71

Macadamia-stuffed chicken drumsticks 68
Mango, with marinated pork kebabs 58
Marinated pork kebabs with mango 58

Mascarpone, with individual orange cakes 121
Melon balls, orange and green in watermelon jelly with zabaglione 129
Mushrooms, with porterhouse steak 51
Mustard marinated steak with red and yellow peppers 48

Nectarines, grilled, with baked ricotta 116

Ocean trout with baby bok choy 95
Octopus coriander baby, with grilled mussels 102
Orange and green melon balls in watermelon jelly with zabaglione 129
Orange, individual cakes with mascarpone 121

Palmina's charcoal eggplants and tomatoes 20
Panettone with blackberries, raspberries and strawberries 126
Panzanella 6
Penne with eggplant, spinach and tomato 23
Peppers
   long green, and asparagus 28
   red and yellow, with mustard marinated steak 48
   with eggplant, zucchini and roast chicken 74
   rosemary and garlic-stuffed lamb with spinach and red pepper sauce 44
   stuffed long green 31
Pina's artichoke frittata 32
Pork
   fillets with zucchini and carrots 57
   marinated kebabs with mango 58
Porterhouse steak with mushrooms 51
Prawns
   ginger and coriander, with rocket and cucumber salad 108
   grilled, with mint and ginger 107

Quail, grilled, with herbs and cucumber salad 78

Rack of lamb with eggplants and rosemary walnut pesto 41
Ricotta
   baked, with grilled nectarines 116
   with chicken breast and spinach 64
   cream filled cones 118
   with grilled vegetables on rocket 24
Roast chicken served with eggplant, zucchini and peppers 74
Roast duck with cavulisceddi and caramelised apple 81
Rocket
   and cucumber salad with ginger and coriander prawns 108
   and ricotta with grilled vegetables 24
   with chicken liver, orange, and pomegranate salad 12

Salad of parsley-crumbed baby vegetables 14
Sardines grilled, with walnuts and Italian oak lettuce and olive salad 99
Sausages
   Italian, with apples and hazelnuts 52
   Italian, with garlic and rosemary roast potatoes 55
Scallops grilled, with artichokes 105
Seafood, antipasti of chargrilled, with vegetables 110
Snowpeas, with grilled trevally and tomatoes 90
Spatchcock, spicy, with avocado salad 76
Spicy spatchcock with avocado salad 76
Stuffed long green peppers 31
Sweet potato mashed, with grilled duck and yellow beans 82

Tomato
   Palmina's charcoal, and eggplants 20
   penne with eggplant and spinach 23
   with eye fillet, oregano and boiled potatoes 47
Trevally
   grilled, with roast potatoes 89
   grilled, with snow peas and tomatoes 90
Trout, ocean, with bok choy 95
Tuna grilled, with eggs and capers 96

Whiting, King George, with salsa verde and roast potatoes 92

Zucchini and carrots, with pork fillets 57